The Names
Leave the Stones

For
Pine Grove
Sisters

The Names
Leave the Stones

POEMS NEW AND SELECTED

Steven Michael Berzensky

COTEAU BOOKS
WWW.COTEAUBOOKS.COM

Edited by Catherine Hunter.

Cover painting by Marc Chagall, *Lovers at the Bridge,* 1948
© Estate of Marc Chagall/SODRAC (Montreal) 2001.

Author photo by Hugh Mullin.
Cover and book design by Duncan Campbell.

Printed and bound in Canada at Houghton Boston, Saskatoon.

National Library of Canada Cataloguing in Publication Data

Berzensky, Steven Michael.
The names leave the stones

Poems.
ISBN 1-55050-191-7

I. Title.
PS8553.U695N35 2001   C811'.54   C2001-911218-1
PR9199.3.B41647N35 2001

1   2   3   4   5   6   7   8   9   1 0

COTEAU BOOKS   AVAILABLE IN THE US FROM
401-2206 Dewdney Ave.   General Distribution Services
Regina, Saskatchewan   4500 Witmer Industrial Estates
Canada   S4R 1H3   Niagara Falls, NY 14305-1386

The publisher gratefully acknowledges the financial assistance of the
Saskatchewan Arts Board, the Canada Council for the Arts, the Government
of Canada through the Book Publishing Industry Development Program
(BPIDP), and the City of Regina Arts Commission, for its publishing program.

In memory of my mother and father

and with gratitude
to all my relatives
and friends

Table of Contents

DOCUMENTS

BONECLOUDS

SOLO

THE GRASS SWIMMER

SOMETIMES THE PRAIRIE

UNDER THE WHITE HOOD

This Imagined Garden

Veil

On an autumn day in 1983, tired and hot and six months pregnant, I was passing through Regina, the city of my own birth, during a long journey west. I was in need of sleep, and my travelling companion took me to the home of a friend who lived near the Regina bus depot. Thus I met Mick Burrs, a friendly, smiling host, who let me rest in the cool shade of his apartment, surrounded by towering stacks of cardboard cartons. As I drifted off to sleep, I vaguely wondered what could possibly be in all those boxes....

Time passed. Things changed. My baby was born, grew up, and is out tonight shopping for a graduation dress. Over the years, I've met with Mick many times in many places. He has changed his name to Steven Michael Berzensky. As for me, I found out what was in all those boxes. Poems!

A lot of poems! By the summer of 2000, when we started this project, Mick had published close to 700 poems in various places, including five volumes of poetry and countless chapbooks, so there was plenty to choose from, most of it so good that the task was a challenge—and the reading was sheer pleasure.

Stepping into the world of these poems is like awakening again and again to the simple wonder of reading and writing. I love "Boy and Book," where the sound of the pages turning is like a gentle but insistent summons, "as if a cat had been left outside and,/at intervals, was scratching on the door," and "The Mysteries of Sex," where the falling snow resembles surreal commas, semi-colons, and question marks. Other poems honour the lives and work of Anne Szumigalski, Pat Lowther, and Eli Mandel. And in a triumphant act of resurrection, "Osip's Last Poetry Reading" imagines the "luminous plumes" of breath emanating from the doomed poet Osip Mandelstam, as he reads aloud for the last time. These poems remind us that writing is magical. It is an act of commemoration, a way of lifting the dead from oblivion, a recognition of what's holy.

But Mick's poems always honour the material world, even as they liberate us from it. They are grounded in history, voiced with a genuine concern for the future of the planet and a straightforward hatred of the fascist violence that threatens to destroy us. From the swimming pools of Encino, California, to the lush forests of British Columbia, to the windswept prairie, the poet observes, appreciates, and records in vivid detail the beauty of the natural world, the vitality of family and friends, the strength of the human spirit, and sometimes—as in "Veil"—our terrible fragility. (After seven years, even if I'm simply skimming through it for errant commas, "Veil" still has the power to make me weep.)

This collection, as a whole, has the power to change the way I see the world when I'm inside it. In fact, I can't remember, any more, the Mick I first met in 1983. His image wavers in memory. What I remember now are the words, the images, the world of the books through which I glimpse him. Here in Berzensky's world, every mote and molecule is alive and breathing. Nothing stays still for long. Writing commemorates, but it never reifies. It transforms. Question marks drift from the clouds like sparkling crystals of snow. Luminous plumes of breath rise into the starry sky. The names leave the stones. It's true. They peel themselves from the cold marble and float free of what they were. Leaving us to imagine them.

Catherine Hunter
Winnipeg, Manitoba, 2001

HEART

it is always becoming a poem
this furnace, this fire
in a corner of the body's dark

this is the place that burns
whatever has been broken

Against the Wind

*In the voice of my great-grandfather, Philip Levi. He was born
Philip Denovitch in Vilna, Lithuania, circa 1862; and he died
in the Jewish Home for the Aged, Indianapolis, Indiana, in
1955. At his death he was believed to be at least 92 or 93 years
old, but no one knows for certain.*

THE PEACH TREE

After my sweet Rachel died
I lived among the old smells
in our house on Union Street

among the sour cabbage leaves
simmering on our gas stove
and the sharp-scented bar of ivory soap
wet like snow in the basin
beside our four-legged bathtub
and the clustered mothballs hanging
with my threadbare jackets and shirts
in our dark bedroom closet

I had no bedpan then
no coffinwood cane
no wheelchair
only my miniature whiskey bottles
that I sampled every day
and my long Havana cigars
and my pocket watch
with its silver chain
and my peach tree in the yard

In summer I picked the peaches
to store in the icebox
and now and then

bit into one, alone

Iron

Max, my son, was already dying
when I stopped going to the yard
Philip Levi and Son
Buyers & Processors
of Scrap Iron & Metal

I was in my eighties then

All my relatives agreed
it was not good for my back
to work, to strain

No one checked out
what was good for my soul

I had always believed
whenever someone casts away
a thing considered useless

God sees
that someone else
might still make use of it

this is one of His hopeful Laws
of Creation
            of Salvage

for centuries in Europe
my devout kin
had to become

peddlers, merchants, brokers

to withstand
the iron barbs
of unrelenting hatred

to feed their children
something more than bitter herbs

how the innocent must everywhere
learn some cold craft of cleverness
to survive

            The last day
I unlocked the door
to our redbricked shop
(iron bars on the windows)

and unlocked the fencegate
to our scrapyard

the old winch truck
we had always relied on
was still parked there
as if it were waiting
to drive one of us around
(Max or I)
where we would hoist

the iron from the motley
piles of cast-off machinery, the twisted
rods, the discarded beams and pipes, the obsolete
transformers, the used batteries from wrecked
cars and trucks, the iron

camouflaged by grease and grime
that always spoke to me
of the only true alchemy

how something cold and black
could be turned into gold
first cut by our torches
then reshaped into smaller pieces
for the smelting furnaces
at the great chimneyed mills

       The last day
I turned over in my bed,
turned over
       our ring of keys
to a man not in our family

and turned my back
on this, my back
that had become

heavy as iron, my back

that had nothing
to do with this
anymore

I had slowed down,
that's all

       slowed down

GREATGRANDSON

One day they brought Mickey (Shirley's boy)
with his halo of dark curly hair
over to my house
the only time I remember him
visiting me there

He stood so far away from me
behind the screen door
was afraid to come near
shadows
the barriers between us

So I walked over to him
the slats of the wooden floor
resounding with my slow steps
as I slapped over them in my slippers

and handed the boy a peach
I had picked from my tree

He would not eat it

and in his brown eyes
I could see

I was only
a strange little man
with a three-day beard
that scratched

when I bent down
to kiss his cheek

THE FEEDING

Go ahead put your plastic
straw to my lips
don't ask me
anymore
if I might want

to feed myself
You won't let me

chew my food
it's applesauce
and orange juice and

porridge again

There is something dark
at the back
of your eyes

waiting to relieve you
of me

I treated
my cold scrap iron
with more respect

than you dear nurse
feeding this old flesh

VOICE

It has become a blade
sliding through a dull sharpener

all it can do is scrape the wind

it gurgles and coughs and
spits

it scratches words in air

it sandpapers
the already brittle

walls of my throat

STANZAS FOR MY GRANDMOTHER

For Anna Rosenberg Levi
1886-1977

GREY BORDERS I

Like you who would become
the mother of my mother,
your family running from the burning villages
on the grey border between Poland and Lithuania;

like my father in 1905, his family slipping out
of czarist Russia, under the shadows of night;
his father wearing a conscript uniform, but this
no defence against terror, dreaming of passage,

four on a boat sailing toward Paradise;
like the ancient Hebrews, fleeing the whips
of slavery and the Pharaoh's troops, fleeing
groaning Egypt; I too would experience

the bitter taste of Exodus, leaving the land
where I was born, crossing the grey border
that stretched across a peaceful continent,
no peace in my war-resisting heart.

GREY BORDERS 2

You could not understand why your grandson
fled the country that was your refuge,
left the land of freedom—to be free!

Not to struggle in someone else's war,
not to kill or be killed, but to find

the gift of poetry
along paths in northern woods,
songs waiting to drop like red berries

from the arms
of snow-clad trees.

GREY BORDERS 3

I had not seen you for fourteen years.

Now at the grey border separating our lives
the bus driver turned the motor off—
and I watched an officer step aboard.

He walked like a sober undertaker
slowly down the aisle—
to go through luggage,
question each passenger one by one:

birthplace,
identification,
reason for this journey.

He stopped at my seat.
Would I be allowed to return,
visit you in your ninetieth year?
I was told to step off the bus

into the front office:
grey and barren,
except for the framed photograph
(colours fading) of a smiling President.

It was a brief interrogation.
Someone took my name down
then entered another room,
closing the door behind him.

Ordered back to the bus,
I waited below the long rack
that held my guitar

in its zippered black case,
waited like a condemned man.
But when they waved

the bus through, across the grey border,
I released my guitar
from its dark coffin

and sang to the sunlight.

THE DOOR

I returned to my city of summer.
I informed no one I would be coming,
not even you (who always knew before).

At the reception desk I told a nurse
(who was cheerful, burly) not to announce:
Your grandson has arrived from Canada.

She led me up the disinfected stairwell
to your door, and shouted, as I stood behind her,
Mrs. Levi! Someone here to see you!

Only when I walked toward you
were you awakened from your dream:

surprised, weeping.

The Darkened Taxicab

You never told me
if I had visited your dreams
as you had visited mine.

Surprised me.
More than once.
Like that time

on a city street
somewhere inside me
when you stepped out

of a darkened taxicab.
I ran to you
and hugged you.

You smiled.
Said nothing.
When I opened

my eyes to sunlight
you were gone.

THE OLD VILLAGE

In my new country
I live with my roots

hanging from the air.
Did our family
always live this way?

In America, did you yearn
to return to that dark
earth where you were born?

In ninety years
Suwalki, the old village,
your birthplace, had changed

its clothing many times—
each time the blood
of its young and old

had to be wiped away, each time
the blood
on the cold stones,

each time the cleansing
of its wars,
pogroms, tears—

who among us now
would long to go back to that?

The Well

On your bedside table
old photographs of your grandchildren,
myself among them,
not as we are, but as your memory
had posed us, smiling, young forever.

In the sunlight that day
I sat on the edge of your bed.
You let me hold your hand,
warm, thin, blue-veined,
a dying bird's wing.

Can you hear me now?
I speak to you from the well
whose bottom is unknown.

I am finding out
why we are mostly water.

the boy remembers visiting his grandmother
in the city of summer far away

remembers his fearless joy
capturing fireflies one night
around the hedges down the lamplit street

remembers cupping
each firefly in his small hands
to take to sleep with him

how he made
with his grandmother's mason jar
a lantern of their glowing

how brightly
they kept away
the terrors of the night

and he remembers
in the morning when he awoke
how he shook the lantern in his hands

and could not wake

the fireflies, the
pale green fireflies

POEM BEGINNING WITH A PHRASE BY KANDINSKY

In memory of my grandfather
Max Levi, 1883-1954

The thunderclap and the buzzing of mosquitoes
ventured in with the driving rain, stirred
the sticky residue on the plastic tablecloth—
the crumbs of yellow bread, the crushed
bones of fish, the puddles of spilled wine—
and lit up the knives nailed on the kitchen wall,
while the green sky flashed like a neon sign.

The thunderclap and the buzzing of mosquitoes
puffed up the stairs like Anna, aired
their humid bedroom where in shadows he had sat
for years, half of him embracing the other
in paralysis, that confined place where once
in a thunderstorm like this he had urinated
on the floor, his spread fingers shaking in the

dark fumbling unable to reach
the metal pan lit up by lightning flash,
the thunderclap and the buzzing of mosquitoes
merging then with deep summoning moans, rousing
the house's summer visitors, daughter and grandson,
from the guestroom down the hallway. He was
sobbing when Shirley and Mickey came in
and soon washed away the proof,
the baby he had again become.

After he was taken curled and cold
from the chair of his last years
and gently placed into his final bed,
Anna came quietly in, alone, her eyes
sifting through their room's
diminished heritage of dust.

Now Anna is seated at the table
beside the kitchen window; it trembles
in the dark. With her wet palms spread upon
the cloth, her fingers pick at crumbs, at bones.
While the rain labours up the stairs and sweeps
their room again, she hears *the thunderclap
and the buzzing of mosquitoes.*

My Great Aunt Sarah on the living room sofa
looking sorrowful through her smile

That day she took me down into the basement
to show me all the food
she had been saving for years
"for another Great Depression"

shelves and shelves and shelves
of canned peas canned peaches canned creamed corn
her safeguard against starvation
her argument against sorrow

After my Great Aunt Sarah died
the next tenants who moved in
must have been surprised
to find a supermarket in their basement

neat shelves of tin cans
shining like silver from floor to ceiling
her treasure never opened

for Mary Shepperd

It keeps her company while she is here.
Those two stiff arms have embraced her sides.
She can't pry herself loose. She is caught
in the lull of its creaking sway.

Each plank underfoot says: Now you stay put.
Only if she exerts herself will she rise
from her quilt of memories and step further
into the world beyond this room.

The light outside the window beckons, longing
to stroke her with its powdered rays,
to fetch her with its warmth. But she doesn't move.

Except back and forth. She is drifting
to sleep, suspended in space, a passenger
dreaming of moons and rocking chairs.

Old Jewish Cemetery
Indianapolis, Indiana

Daylight. I walk quietly
inside the rusted iron fence
at the end of Kelly Street.
Searching, I step among
uneven rows of marble
inscribed against the wind.

Footsteps on gravel
do not interrupt
my voiceless chanting
of their names:
grandpa Max
grandma Anna
great aunt Sarah
great grandpa Zady.

After every sunset
the names leave the stones
to form a congregation
and wander the flowered paths
in mute, hallowed circles.

I still live above ground
in another country
where no relatives reside.
Now I visit this garden
overgrown with marbled names

where not even memories stay rooted
where every fragile blossom,
every dropped petal, shines.

The dead leave us images of themselves:

Souvenirs in washed-out colours. Dried petals
pressed into family albums. Shadows that stain
our papered walls. They abandon us in our rooms,
teach us how to converse with dust, will not
let us forget them. In our glistening
reeds of dream we try to free ourselves
from their tangled reflections, the memory
of their once green, once brighter air.

They shiver inside us now, not as noisy
leaves shaken by the wind but as thin yellow
shoots, muffled, insistent. Their ceaseless
splash of wings closes in on us. In moonlight:
the small stray feather we find in our hands.

Paradise

in the darkness of her womb
i could not see

i would laugh and swing
eight years old
a pilot taking wing

in our garden shout
bombs over tokyo!

on a swinging crescent
a boy too young to know

bombs are appalling things
tokyo a human place

i only now remember
our japanese gardener
hoeing, turn away his face

THE FABLED BLUE POOLS OF PARADISE

OH-OH YESSS ACROSS the street from us
and behind the alley from us
and over the fence to the left of us
and over the fence to the right of us
in our home in the San Fernando Valley
all day and all night our golden neighbours
laughed and dived into their fabled blue pools of paradise.

WE MOVED TO ENCINO when I was nine years old and it was
the day before my sister Renee's seventh birthday
and we lived in a ranch-style house
in a 25-year-mortgage housing tract
built for the middle class
with three bedrooms and three bathrooms
our backyard lawn littered
with sunbaked dry coils
from our black cocker spaniel
dark walnuts dropped
from our English walnut trees
our house surrounded
on all four sides
by the cool and shining
fabled blue pools of paradise.

WE COULD NOT AFFORD a swimming pool
but my father proudly drove a Cadillac
through the streets of Encino
(the Spanish name for White Oak)
once an immense grove of English walnut trees
bulldozed by developers
to pave the way for the middle class
and only some of the trees survived
refusing to surrender
to the fabled blue pools of paradise.

ENCINO WAS POPULATED at first
by Spanish-speaking missionaries
who gave the place its name
later by English-speaking movie stars
like Al Jolson
grinning as he sat at the parlour piano
eager to sing for his ma
excited to utter Hollywood's
first spoken words for the sparkling screen
and in that Warner Brothers Vitaphone movie
it was his pious papa who wanted Al to be
a cantor not a jazz singer
while the whole world listened
to Jolson's soundtrack of song
(oh how those blue skies smiled at him)
and when the star first erupted in words
he put an end to the reading of lips
and the silence of talk
and the muteness of song /
this was years before
Jolson would serve
as honorary mayor of Encino
and would quietly preside
over its fabled
blue pools of paradise.

THEY EACH OWNED a private rancho in Encino
Al Jolson   Roy Rogers & Dale Evans
John (the Duke) Wayne   Clark (the King) Gable
all these famous movie stars
our eminent neighbours / among them Bud Abbott
whose estate housed a large gun collection
including the hunting rifle
rumoured to belong to Adolf Hitler
that real-life villain of the 30s and 40s
whose favourite movie turned out to be
a monster epic manufactured in Hollywood /
and I sat next to freckled Bud Abbott Junior
in my fifth grade class at Encino Elementary
and one sunny morning he brought to school
a black-and-white Abbott & Costello
feature-length film and Mrs. McFarlane pulled down
the shades and turned off the lights and switched on
the projector and we all roared as we watched
thin Abbott Senior & chubby Costello comically escape
the sinister clutches of Lon Chaney Junior & Bela Lugosi
and across from me in the same class sat tall Cheryl Rogers
daughter of the Republic's Roy Rogers & Dale Evans
and at another table sat a boy named Basil
whose father helped manage Bing Crosby Enterprises
for the world-famous crooner who had starred
in many Paramount movies
including *Blue Skies*
where it was Bing's turn
to sing of the days as they hurried by
with those breezy white clouds
flying above each fabulous blue
pool of paradise.

ROY ROGERS REVERED TRIGGER his golden
palomino and so did not bury him
had him stuffed and mounted for display
after the dependable horse had died of old age
and Roy and the Duke and the King
rarely walked the streets with their guns
flashing in their holsters and rarely drove down
the palm tree boulevards in their Cadillacs
and I saw only one of them once
in the flesh   off the screen
MGM's Gable (the King)
who had played the hero in *Gone with the Wind*
the year before I was born
and who looked just like my father
they both had black moustaches
and were heavy-set
but the King wore dark glasses
that morning when he stepped out
of the Encino post office
with some letters in his hand
and I glowed
in that flickering light for hours
there among my glorious neighbours
who could rarely be seen
as they swam
in their fabled blue pools of paradise.

THE LAST TIME I saw my father
he and my mother had come up to Canada
to visit me in Vancouver
two years after I had fled the Golden State
had voted *No!* with my body
to the bloodletting in Vietnam
and my father and I sat beside each other
on the motel-room bed
(my mother had chosen the armchair)
one block away from the grey waters of English Bay
where we watched colour television
The Jolson Story starring Larry Parks
who was banished from Hollywood forever
(a few years after the movie was made)
for admitting he once was a Communist
and who artfully mouthed
the words Al Jolson sang
including "The Anniversary Waltz"
my father and mother's favourite song
(O yes the night they were wed
how they danced how they danced)
and now before *The Jolson Story* was over
I turned to tell my father
(between commercials) that despite everything
I still loved him
but he pretended he didn't hear
as we sat with our iced soft drinks
against the motel-room pillows
watching Jolson sing
through the lips of Larry Parks /
and it was awkward
always had been
after the glow of my infancy

when I was the curly-haired prince in his eye
he on his back on the grass in the park
holding me above his head
tossing me skyward
my laughter infectious
until we had become (in the undoing
of time) mirrors of one another
mirrors that had lost their silver
to reflect only our defects
in his eyes the son
who did not turn out to be
the son he had desired
athlete   hero   businessman   lawyer
and in my eyes the father
who was not
the father I wished him to be
accepting accepting
accepting of me (and now
only our soiled distortions
were greeting us here)
but O
the night of the day
they were wed in Hollywood
my father and mother
imagined they were movie stars
imagined they were Fred Astaire and Ginger Rogers
as they danced around and around
one of the fabled blue pools of paradise.

AND NONE OF US realized that last night
in the motel room in Vancouver
how one year later
these two Als
my father the sign painter and real estate broker
Jolson the movie star and popular singer
would share
the same consecrated hillside
a green park in the grey smog
of the City of Angels
each with his place under the grass
(though they had never met
on the palm tree boulevards of Encino)
and how their grey hair
would slowly intertwine
with the holy roots
in the dark soil of Hollywood
(near the oil derricks and bright roar
of the city's congested freeways)
and how the last audience of their bones
would only hear the stillness
of talk and the silence of song
from a million flickering stars

light years removed
from all the fabled blue pools
of paradise.

we are walking bundles
of electric impulses
the light in each other's eyes

we are warm hearts
in cold ribcages
each body
a portable prison
until we touch one another
conspiring to escape

we are God's fingertips
stroking the dark universe

Documents

WHITE HANDKERCHIEFS

California   El Dorado   The Golden State
The Gilded One   City of Gold
Country of Fabulous Wealth

*"There are simply too many guns in American closets and
cabinets, waiting to go off."*— AMERICAN NOTES,
CANADIAN EDITION, TIME MAGAZINE

This poem is about
my father and his cool black revolver
among the many houses
in sunny California's San Fernando Valley
equipped with a gun—a handgun procured
wherever friendly firearms dealers are found.
Why did my father need to purchase
the minimal American arsenal? (Note: Smile
at your neighbours, but always
bolt your door.)

My father had a gluttony.
For FRONT PAGE DETECTIVE.
A monthly thirst.
For TRUE POLICE CASES.
And a gift subscription.
To TRUE DETECTIVE.
That I gave to him on request for his 58th birthday.

In the master bedroom
he kept a cool black revolver
in the top drawer of his dresser
among his white cotton handkerchiefs
all monogrammed
A.A.B.

The bullets were stationed right next to the revolver
in a small gold-leaf box with Prussian blue lettering.
The shells rattled next to each other once when I
looked into the drawer and tilted the box among
the white handkerchiefs to see
if it would explode.

My father
had a spectator's interest
in violence.

Reclining on a sofa with his feet as well as his head
propped comfortably on cushions and with a pair of
reading spectacles perched on his nose he would be
an eyewitness to the detailed and graphic reports
of blood and gore and suspicion
and detection and arrest and confession
collected and stapled together and
distributed monthly to local magazine stands
across the gun-toting land
with the inevitable blonde beauty bound
and threatened with a knife
or a noose or a gun
by a sneering male malcontent
on each glossy cover.

On some nights a single branch
on one of our English walnut trees
would scrape the master bedroom window.
What if that branch was a burglar
scratching to break inside?

My father
always felt safer
when he remembered his cool black revolver
sleeping among his white cotton handkerchiefs.

I. Of Names And Numbers

S
is for secrecy, S is for
Sam as in samovar, S is for Steven,
his first name

M
is for Mick or Mickey, from Micha-el
(who is like God?), the prince of angels,
his middle name

B
is for Burrs, from Berzinsky
(son of one who lives near birches?),
his family name

the family name changed to Burrs
by the father, in the New World,
to fit in with the Smiths,
to be more acceptable to the Browns

[the name changed, once more,
to Berzensky, by the son,
55 years after he was born,
hoping to achieve some cryptic regard]

and this poem
is written in memory
of Sam Berzinsky, the grandfather
Albert Arthur Burrs, the father

Sam Berzinsky,
who died two years before the grandson was born,
who Steven Michael was named after
[according to the ancient naming tradition]

Sam Berzinsky, conscript
of the czar, dealer in plumbing fixtures,
born April 20, 1875, Kiev, Ukraine, Old Russia,
died only four days before his 63rd birthday
April 16, 1938, Chicago, Illinois, the New World

Albert Arthur Burrs,
who was named after Alex Berzinsky,
the great-grandfather, of whom
nothing is now known

Albert Arthur Burrs, painter
of signs, buyer and seller of land,
born August 1, 1902, Kiev, Ukraine, Old Russia,
died seven months after his 65th birthday
February 3, 1968, Encino, California, the New World

Steven Michael Berzensky
has written this poem February 4, 1983,
in Regina, Saskatchewan, the New World,
15 years after the death of the father
[and revised the poem January 21, 2001,
in Yorkton, Saskatchewan, the New World,
33 years after the death of the father]

Steven Michael Berzensky, maker
of images, composer of songs
[conceived in love by the father
and mother, Shirley Levi Burrs,
during the first week of July, 1939,
nine weeks before the beginning of World War Two]

Steven Michael Berzensky, first and last son,
archivist of names, chronicler of numbers,
born 37 years after the birth of the father,
65 years after the birth of the grandfather,
April 10, 1940, Los Angeles, California, the New World

Los Angeles,
Spanish for the Angels

date of death, one more
secret God keeps

II. Of The Unknown And Unseen

Of the one who I was named after
and never met:
all that I possess,

three images and a certificate:
County of Cook, City of Chicago,
signed by Dr. Charles Berkovitz

with principal cause
and contributing causes
of death:

carcinomous colon
carcinomatous cachexia
acute pulmonary edema / and

the first image: he is standing alone
in baggy trousers and a white
sleeved shirt buttoned at the neck,

his sleeves are rolled up to the elbows,
his thumbs tug on both suspenders,
an unlit cigar is pinched in his right hand;

behind him, the brick wall of a warehouse
glares in the sunlight, no windows; before him,
on the other side of a low wire fence,

the grass grows sparsely among the weeds;
my grandfather, in this image, is almost bald,
is smiling, or perhaps, talking to the imagemaker,

or he is whistling a secret song, his mouth
shaped into the lyrical letter O

the second image: he does not appear
among the many shadows of poplars and
birches as they cool the tall

headstones in a Jewish cemetery in Chicago;
in this image his is the smallest headstone,
etched with the dates of his birth and death,

his face framed in a sealed O above his name,
his headstone partly obscured by a hedge
growing beside it; and in the distance

a woman, dark-haired, bends over a grave,
laying an unseen bouquet, or wreath, upon it

the third image: he is holding
an empty glass in his right hand, is seated
near the brass samovar on a circular table
draped by a dark tasselled floral cloth,

and his right hand is the one
closest to the spigot of the samovar,
where he is seated third from the left,
he, without a beard but a thin moustache

that angles down past both corners of his
upper lip, he, the young man in the centre
among twelve others, all cavalrymen,
all posing solemnly in their caps and

uniforms and long black boots, each
seated or standing or reclining with
an empty glass in his hand, each with
at least one o-shaped medallion on his tunic;

his head is the only one tilted, relaxed,
his eyes gazing somewhere unknown, unseen,
past the shrouded imagemaker,
through the shrouded years

unable
to tell me his dream
unable to tell me

the secret he keeps.

III. OF BLOOD AND BONES AND BARBED WIRE:
     MISSING PERSONA REPORT

some historical fragments:

*1962. The officials of Kiev renewed their undertaking at Babi
Yar. Bulldozers continued to turn up bones that had become
entwined in barbed wire. Babi Yar was soon eradicated. In
addition, the old Jewish cemetery nearby was finally levelled...
then replaced by a television centre constructed on its grounds.*
—PARAPHRASE OF DATA FROM "BABI YAR'S LEGACY," AN
ARTICLE WRITTEN BY LUCY S. DAWIDOWICZ, *The New York
Times Magazine*, SEPTEMBER 27, 1981

a documentary approach:

*"Write (a) poem/article...w/footnotes...form objective, partly
lyrical..."*—MARGINAL NOTE BY ANDREW SUKNASKI, POET,
JOTTED ON HIS COPY OF THE ABOVE DOCUMENT WHICH HE
GRACIOUSLY SHARED WITH ME FOR RESEARCH PURPOSES,
AUGUST, 1988

a personal interpretation:

these missing persons this missing persona these missing
shadows from the life of one body the body of one life

1.

my grandfather Sam Berzinsky
who died in 1938
the year before my conception
[his secrets buried with his bones]

who I was named after in 1940
the year of my birth
[his blood seeping through my body]

whose hand never held my own
[I summon his image inscribed on stone]

2.

my great-grandfather Alex Berzinksy
whose name I never knew
until I was forty years old (1980)

whose date of birth
and date of death
have been removed
from all accounts

whose bones
were likely buried
in the old Jewish cemetery in Kiev
beside the victims of a chain of pogroms

my father did not speak of him
or of the pogrom in 1905
that pushed my father's family
across the sea to North America

was he, my great-grandfather,
a fatality
of one of those massacres?

I will never know

3.

my father Albert Arthur Berzinsky
once was two years old

too young to be told
every legal intricacy
of persecution and hate

as he slept in the arms
of my grandfather
who could no longer wait

to desert the Czar's army
and the sanctioned
massacres of the state

4.

later I too would escape
my country of birth
as my grandfather and father
had escaped their own

my vanishing act of 1965
occurred sixty years after
they had fled their homeland

I slipped away from the state
the one they had escaped to

the state that now registered
my body as its own

I absconded with
my blood my bones

I ran off
with the prayers of my ancestors
churning in my soul

fear driving me
dreams of paradise
urging me onward

my role as exile
in perfect keeping
with our family history

5.

Alex Berzinsky's bones
were not allowed to rest
in the soil of Ukraine

I believe this is what happened
to the remains of my great-grandfather:

how his cold blood underground
later was joined
by the warm red stream

of thousands of others
slaughtered in a ravine nearby (1941)
the year after I was born

the bodies of entire families
sanctified by bullets

their bones blessed and bulldozed

in mud and barbed wire
by the Nazi elite
(Sonderkommando Unit 4A, Einsatzgruppe C)

in that grim and hungry mouth
known as Babi Yar

6.

finally in peacetime
by state directives (1962)
the old Jewish cemetery in Kiev
and my great-grandfather's name
were obliterated

this progressive act
required only
the word of authority
the collaboration of silence

how the "final solution"
found perfection in Kiev
concocted by invaders from another land
completed later by the local regime

and condoned by those who could hide
behind the whitewashed walls
of their simple piety

this serviceable cancellation this
unconscious scrubbing
implies

no Jewish child ever breathed
on the slate of memory
in Russia or Ukraine

and since no gravestone
displays his name
my great-grandfather

never existed on this earth

7.

now you know why
I do not exist

but at least you know
who I am

a missing persona

an image in your brain

I am the blood
and the bones
and the barbed wire

the names and the names and
the names

of my ancestors in Kiev
where my father and my grandfather
and my great-grandfather
were born

where many bodies
now rest in pieces

under the modern communications centre
erected by the state

and today
(it is official)

the state announces:

let all good citizens
take note

death
and history

have been
replaced

by television

thinking
and remembering

are no longer
required.

IV. OF IMAGES AND ILLUSIONS:
UNLIKE FATHER, UNLIKE SON

I am left only with images. Graphic tricks of memory.
Illusions. And each one clashes with later reality. Unlike
father, unlike son.

The first image: my father at the train depot in Los Angeles
in the late 1920s. He looks as slim then as I am now & have
been most of my life. And he's immaculately tailored, so
people would say. While I was growing up, Dad had dozens
of suits, countless ties, many pairs of shoes lined up in his
wardrobe closet. Now I wear the same scuffed shoes every
day until they wear out. You'll rarely see me in a suit & tie.
Tieless I am & shall remain.

In later years Dad took on an uncanny resemblance to the
movie star Clark Gable, moustache & all. Image of a big
man, his shadow swallowing mine when he snaps my
picture. Now I stand outside his shadow. Or I need to think
I do.

Image before I was born: my smiling father in a Hollywood
cowboy outfit riding a stuffed horse & shooting a pistol in
front of painted clouds. Un-American, I vowed long ago I
would never own a gun.

Later image of my dad holding a chubby trusting laughing
infant upside down above the hard ground. Or like a master
illusionist suspending him by only two fingers in thin but
fabulous air.

Another image of my father: crouched, posing under a gangster's brimmed hat, cigar in one hand, me leaning against his knee. In this image I am five or six, my father is forty-three. No indication here he would soon bellow at me for my inability to tie my shoelaces following his crescendo of exasperated instructions. No sign here I would soon learn to stutter. No sign here I would catch the whooping cough, a seemingly incurable case. No sign here I would then be sent away to health camp in the mountains for my own good.

Beyond these images, did my father perceive his son's eventual & lone desire to sing?

[This father, this son
lived in parallel universes

where, at first, they
brightly mirrored one another

until, finally,
they survived as contraries.]

V. Of The Living And The Dead: Reasons Why I Did Not Attend My Father's Funeral

Because I imagine no one would notice my father
walking among them. They would be too busy
with the preparations: the choosing
and purchasing of the gravesite,
the rewriting of the will in their heads.
The living only notice themselves burying the dead.

Because someone might see me sneaking in:
Why are you so calm? Why don't you cry?
Don't you care about your father?
You ought to be ashamed, swearing
at our government at a time like this.
Behave yourself. Others are watching.

Because of the imagined eulogy, with its quasi-
biblical twist, which now I would not have to sit through:
May the father (Abraham) at last find eternal rest.
Earth was his while he was here.
He sacrificed himself for (Isaac) his son
who chose to be absent during his father's last years.

Because in reality, the secular son
by staying away at least would not desecrate
his father's death. But (isn't it strange?)
the one who conspicuously was not there
still dreams of the one who died,
still remembers him with complicated intensity.

Because I play Hamlet to my father's ghost
and I fear my father's enemy
who I must continue to pursue
and I know the pursued may be the pursuer—
since father and son had never reconciled,
could never completely accept the other.

Because I became the voluntary exile
the one who fancied himself a poet
penning diatribes to his father
against wars and against fathers
who sent their sons to war.

Because other fathers of other sons
vowed if any draft-dodging beatnik
should ever cross that border
during their latest righteous war—
he would be arrested and jailed.

Because it turned out, during our own war,
my father died of multiple wounds
before either of us learned
how to surrender, unconditionally,
into the resolute arms of the other.

I still dream about my father
who I've not seen for many years.
His body sleeps beneath the dark
in soil indifferent to his fate.

Awake, I do not wish to see
what became of him:
how his bones outgrew
his flesh, how his blood stopped
flowing into tears, into laughter.
Yet in the sunlit yard of my skull

he lives, bending down
to show me seedlings
from which tall trees will grow
one day to sprout above us all.

Boneclouds

After his father died, his mother remarried: now he returns to their renovated kitchen, sunlight shining on the wet linoleum floor with its new pattern, its mosaic of squares.

His mother had deposited their memories in the desk drawer beneath the telephone. After all these years the grown child stands alone in the dream's warm stroking light, rummaging through the drawer, finding it difficult to shut

because it is stuffed with airmail letters, blank penny postcards, notes in blue ink on slips of pastel paper, family photos, darkened negatives, scenes on the beach, colours faded, faces blurred. When he spots

the word *strokes*
handprinted across the drawer—
he recalls each disease that felled
the giant who was his father—

and he recalls how, unyielding, he became a poet, sliding past his father's wishes. Now the sun feels too hot, a killer dropping through the clouds, popping through the ozone hole.

The telephone rings.
He awakes.
No one answers.

The kitchen is empty.
The telephone has melted down.
The past is over.

Always there is meaning after no meaning, always a pattern emerges: lovers stroke each other's skin, someone else is born, dressed in blood, swimming up into air.

After another interval of darkness this giddy montage begins again: nostalgia dreams, renovation dreams, images in astounding light. They are juxtaposed, they are overexposed: parents and their children, the living and the dead, each spirit's eternal restlessness.

Now some unknown poet scrawls the next sacred text, cave wall jottings, strokes of brilliance, revising the world from the inside out.

[A Short Story in Verse]

> *"My feet are killing me."*
>
> *"What else do I have*
> *to do except complain?"*
>
> *"It's hell growing old."*
>
> — SHIRLEY BARAN,
> THE POET'S MOTHER
> IN HER LAST YEARS

I can see you as we talk
not the thousand miles that separate us
not my own apartment in the cold vast north
but you alone in your big apartment down south
the palm trees swaying outside your windows.

I can see your sore feet propped
on a cushion and a towel
upon the glass coffee table
in front of the television set
you had been watching when I called
(the volume now turned down
by the remote you hold).

In your living room
I can see that long white sofa
where you rest every evening—
the sofa once part of our Encino home—
and you have kept
that expensive showpiece all these years.

And Dad's huge oil painting of a circus
is still framed above the sofa—
this whimsical scene the room's highlight
glowing with merriment above your head.

And on glass shelves along the walls—
beside the photographs
of your daughter and her wedding
and your two grandchildren and your son—
you keep doodads and knick-knacks
from your travels after Dad died:
small painted souvenirs, crystal sculptures
paperweights and tall vases
empty of flowers.

When I tell you "Thank you for the gift"
(something I am always grateful for)
you apologize for not sending me
my birthday cheque on time this year—

as if there was something
you had to self-criticize
in such a thoughtful gesture
as if nothing could ever be exactly right
as if love were somehow not enough.

And when I inquire how you are—
hoping to hear some good news for a change—
you tell me your latest medical problems
in intricate and elaborate detail
and the doctors you've been seeing
and the medicine you've been taking.

Sjogren's Syndrome is a new diagnosis.
"How do you spell that?"
I have to write it down.
Now I will add this
to Peripheral Neuropathy and Erythromyalgia
to heart arrhythmia and high blood pressure
and the other ailments you endure.

I ask again: "Mom, what are those medicines you're taking?"

"Coumadin. Dyazide. Premarin. Lanoxin. Halcion.
Sometimes I even forget what does what for which."

"And you're still taking them all?"

"Of course I am! I have to take them.
Or things would be considerably worse."

When I ask you
if you have gone out lately,
you suddenly condemn
your oldest friend in a single sentence:
"She looks like she's at death's door!"

Does this adequately explain
why you don't like to see her anymore
she who is as old as you?
Is her presence a painful reminder
forcing you to look
against your will
into a scuffed and greying mirror?

I am not prepared for further evidence
of this new and grim change in you.
Once more I am stunned into silence.
And I only mutter to myself:

"I wish you wouldn't say
such callous demeaning things
about people who still care about you.
You don't know how it undermines
my love for you. You don't know
how it throws a shroud
over my fondest memories of you."

But you go on to say: "Isn't it sad about
the latest war (halfway around the globe)
and that airplane crash into the sea
and how certain nasty people
are picking on the President"—

and I manage to tell you about my latest project
and you say, "Oh, that's nice, Mickey"—
then you change the subject
as soon as you can
to something you already told me about:
"the terrible heat
I have to put up with in this place."

And I am thinking
"There's something wrong here
something more unsettling
than a Los Angeles earthquake."

But I utter none of this aloud:

"It saddens me to know
the ways you are winding down
the ways you are wearing out.
I would like to tell you
how it might help you feel better
if you chose to speak more gracefully
if you had some kinder things to say.
Yet nothing I say or do
has ever changed your attitude."

And I dare not mention to you anymore
"heaven" or "God" in any form
because you don't want to talk about that.
Once when I asked you why
you said:

"Because it reminds me of *you-know-what!*
And talking about it makes me very upset
do you understand?"

Oh, I understand.
You-know-what.
Yet another name
for *death.*

And so what you say
does not match what you do.
And what you do does not
match what you possess.
And who you are is not the twin
of who you were.

Now you are inertia and momentum
new habits you cannot control
as you, frightened, obedient
stumble forward, a patient
drugged by doctors into darkness.
(They do not know what else
to do with you, other ways you can survive.)

I would like to say:
"Sometimes you leave me baffled
although sometimes I think you're wise.
But you hardly laugh anymore—
and there is something unnerving
fervently chilling in that.

"You are my mother, so I
still believe you deserve compassion
that same compassion you now begrudge
those who've been close to you all these years.

"Yet when I'm talking to you I seem to lose
my ability to articulate
my own passions, my own concerns—
feeling dashed and inundated by yours.

"And I perceive
you are not comforted anymore
by the sunny embrace of my words."

Who, I want to ask,
is the self-effacing parent now—
and who the child to be indulged
for inappropriate behaviour?

But now you tell me you are tired
and I say "okay"—then mercifully
at last (by mutual consent)
both north and south hang up.

But at first I cannot move
from my chair in the kitchen.

When I finally stand
I watch my own shadow fall
spreading its dark blood
across the unswept floor.

eyes closed, face wrinkled,
you take a journey on your haloed pillow

you are a child grown very old and pale
dreaming among your fragile boneclouds
of the heaven you have always longed for

1.

Some of the things she wants me to do
do not need to be done—
or cannot be done.

My mother coming out of sleep
while I wait in the armchair by her bedside:

"I need to get dressed," she announces.
Her first words are uttered to the air.
I only happen to be there to overhear.

"Mom," I say, "you *are* dressed."

Indeed, under the blanket
she is wearing one of her favourite sweaters.
She looks at me quizzically,
then lifts the blanket to check.
Now she sees her sweater
sequined and buttoned warmly around her.

Her surprise is genuine.

Less than a minute later, she whispers:
"Mickey, will you do me a favour?
Will you go downstairs for me?"
[But Mom is downstairs: Room 136, Bed One]
"And tell my doctor—
you know, she's the only woman doctor here."
[Her doctor lives on the other side of town]
"Tell her I am ready to get dressed."

I have to remind my mother, she *is* dressed.
But again that quizzical look
followed by:

"Oh.
      Right.
            I am."

2.

Her need seemed urgent—
until she realized
there was no need.

Are we all programmed
to need and need and need?

And do each of us invent
a need where none exists
simply to fill

this enormous space for needs?

3.

How my mother confronts the silences
near the end of her life:

With needs, real and imagined,
momentous and endlessly recurring—

Until she will need no more,
stilled by darkness, dressed for heaven.

january 11, 1998—evening

like a poem, death
is not something automatic—
it goes through trial and error, then a final draft

    the endless rounds of pain had ceased—
    her suffering stopped when her breath broke free

    we entered her room after they called us—
    her eyes were closed, her mouth left open

    flesh not yet cold, she was all inward now,
    the final secret known at last—but one
    she would not share with us

    how loud her silence, how still her face—
    the air soft around her
    made our memories more intense

    I imagine this—somehow she could see our sorrow,
    son and daughter, ghostly figures at her side

    and if she travelled far enough, then she
    arrived at her own beginning—in clear light

but when I dreamed of her eleven days later
she stepped out of the shadows—confused,
needing my reassurance

I was surprised to find what the living must do—
comfort the dead, reach out to them
whisper words of peace

Solo

midnight, in a warm corner of the living room
beneath the solitary lamp, the boy in pyjamas
about to enter a world different from this one
familiar with its pungent summer smells
(the steamy air, the tasselled purple carpet,
the old mahogany chair, the sticks of spearmint
chewing gum in the green bowl on the table)

alone on the bottom shelf of the glass case,
orphaned, all its meaning hidden, a book,
until the boy reaches in to pick it up
and befriend the pages, place his hands
around the spine and lift that dark
leathered memory belonging to someone else,
bring it close to his own heart

the boy ready to give that abandoned life
more meaning than his own, intending
to occupy this shadowed place for awhile,
this room in his grandmother's house
while she sleeps upstairs and the world sleeps
and there is only once upon a time,
but this time the first time for him

he, one of two conspirators, no longer
strangers, more like secret companions,
and the only sounds boy and book can bear:
the whispering of the clock on the top shelf
and the turning, now and then, of a page
as if a cat had been left outside and,
at intervals, was scratching on the door

BLINDS

In my room, only one lamp
where the motes fall like snow.

Outside, he and his wife
take their nightly walk
under the street lamps.
I know they are outside walking.
Their dog always barks.

Sometimes I've looked
down at them in the dark,
my fingers bending back
the cold snapping blinds.

SNOW

Tonight, I don't get up from my bed.
I rest my head against the wall,
the map where I've leaned for years.
I stare at the black headlines,
the newspaper straddling my legs.

I picture the man, tall, old, blind,
walking stiffly along the snow-covered street,
walking under the street lamps,
never stepping out of the shadows before his eyes.

I picture their ritual. She, leaning
against his shoulder, holding his arm.
He, gripping the leash.
Their dog straining and pulling
in front of them as they walk.

Their dog barks at all things that move.
Tonight, their shadows in the falling snow.

News

In my room, the light
goes off—has failed
in this part of the city.

But I imagine
it is dark everywhere.
I imagine waves of snow

rolling outside,
down all the streets, one wave
falling upon another.

In the darkness, my fingers
glide over print, my flesh

lifts off the news,
the ink melting

on my fingertips like snow.

in the late 1960s, Vancouver

At first I found myself
walking through a slanting dustmote shower
(ribbed by darkness, stained with light)
on a winding path of unfamiliar solitude,
passing by sitka spruce and broadleaf maples,
tamarack and hemlock, canoe birches and cottonwoods,
towering thick-trunked cedars and Douglas firs
that shaded sawed-off stumps and wind-toppled trees.

I'd close the door to my suite one block away and stride
alone through Stanley Park onto Cathedral Trail.
It took time to realize I was in no mortal danger here.
Soon, on my weekend jaunts, if I met someone walking
in the other direction, I would simply nod or smile.

Sometimes I preferred my rooted and silent companions
to my human family—our voices scrape, cut one another down.
I thought of these woods as my own huge backyard,
no barbed wire fence enclosing the peaceable sanctuary.

As I walked past the trees, some of them centuries old,
I'd rub my tactile vision against their furrowed bark
and listen to the scrunch of my rubber soles
on twigs and gravel, leaves and pine needles,
and hear the sudden chittering of chipmunks and squirrels,
the soothing calls and soft stirrings of birds
hidden in the dense and damp and pungent undergrowth.

The distant hum of cars, trucks, and buses
on the highway to and from Lions Gate Bridge
became one of the first sounds my mind transformed—
mountainous rapids now seeming to plunge
through the city's noisy heart.

Gradually my walks released me from the cage
I had carried with me from another country.
The war I had fought inside for years had become
tangible now, pinpointed on the twisting globe, in a place
so green and steamy, it tangled lives across the sea.

No need to defend my conscience here with fisted words.
I had refused to join the cursing exterminating chorus.
I would not have to yield now to the daily round
of bravado masking sudden tremblings, hidden terrors,
nor wear jungle camouflage smeared with more than sweat,
see bodies startled, snapping, falling like trees.

What I found on this soon familiar curving path
was how my thin shadow could easily accompany my body
in natural harmony with cedars, maples, pines
beneath a sky punctured only by sun and clouds.

And what I could feel was the falling away
of all my bruises, real and imagined,
like brittle leaves slowly merging wet with earth.

THE ALIEN

Regina, Saskatchewan, 1974

1. HOUSEGLOW

I stood outside and heard them singing.
Their melodies lay petals of flowers
before the scented feet of their Lord.

Their voices transported their joy
through windows and through walls
onto the street for those who would hear—
but strangely not comforting me
alone on the front porch beside
forty pairs of shoes, with my guitar
bound in its black case and leaning
against my legs, each string silent.

The sky was cloudy, slate black,
but the street was wet, shimmering
with lamplight and houseglow, each home
keeping its occupants warm, while
trees shivered in the wind, branches
not yet green enough for this season—
holding back, distrusting the climate,
uncertain of spring, of warmth
ever arriving to blossom there.

2. SHADOW

I waited to see when their music would end
and wondered if I should enter their company.

Soon the ceremony of praise was over
and I heard chatter and laughter—
and felt more outside than before.

Without glancing back, I went down
the steps and onto the sidewalk, quick
so that no one would know I was there.

I walked home in the company
of my familiar stark shadow:
he who had kept me waiting outside,
weighted down with his wariness,
my heavy rock, my portable mountain.

He, that part of me, afraid—
no, terrified—to confront
the holy climate of light
that hummed inside to greet me.

Here is where I might,
for a time, have subdued
the mental stench of hell,
and joined the radiant circle
singing the ballad of the joyful self.

Tonight I'm greeted by a constellation of grain moths.
Some pulse their wings against the cabinet's dark
while others sleep, stationary as cold stars.
On the shelves above my warm stove their casings
hang like beads of evening dew on blades of grass.

They rest inside plastic bags of oats and wheat
and crawl between long grains of brown rice
and wait to hover over all my future meals.
My tolerance vanishes. I grab a newspaper,
a new-found method of eradication: the printed word.

I roll up the violent headlines, my poised club.
It takes one hour to spatter the kitchen walls
with their tiny eyes, their crushed wings.
I throw away all the food they've infiltrated,
including the raisins that glisten with white grubs.

I'm no longer hungry. I've eaten my last supper.
I've sentenced myself to be hanged, shot, burned at the stake.
How subtle the differences that divide the prolonged life
of a prosaic dictator relishing his brutalities—and
my brief career as an exterminating poet:

I could not dream in peace where dictators rule.
I'm the lyrical enemy of their icy efficiency.
They enjoy keeping body counts of their slain enemies;
they sleep with revolvers under their pillows.
I own no revolver—yet today I'm every dictator's brother.

I know I did what was necessary. When my victims
return tonight, they'll flutter in the cabinet of my dreams.
Again I shall step forward as their executioner.
Or will the angel asleep deep inside me
reach out and touch their breakable wings?

My kitchen faucet drips
in its rhythmic way—
always waiting
until I turn
the last light off.

The wind howls
outside my bedroom window—
just like it's supposed to
in melodramas.

My radiator
hisses at me—
this
is the only way
it can feel at home.

See, I'm really
not alone at night—
all my companions
sing me to sleep.

One winter morning at five o'clock
in the land of Nod
you receive a phone call from a tenant

"Hey! It's freezing in here!
My plants are dying!
My whole body feels
like I'm living in an icebox!
Jesus! You're the caretaker!
Do something about it!"

Obedient, you crawl out of bed
into your pants
into your slippers
down three flights of stairs
feeling groggy and useless
as a cold cup of coffee

You stand near it
praying for it to go on
for you've never fixed anything
at five in the morning
(You cannot think straight
at five in the morning
having gone to sleep
at three o'clock)

In the freezing basement
the Peerless Furnace
sits there
quiet as an organ
in a corner of a church or synagogue

waiting to be switched on
waiting to boom its fiery music

When you call the plumber
about an hour later
begging his forgiveness
for dragging *him* out of bed
he sighs then prods you for details

When you tell him you don't understand
what's wrong with the damned thing
he asks you about the pilot lights
You answer, "Well, two of the three
are still on."

He tells you, *"That's* the problem!"
"What's the problem?" you say

"One of the pilot lights," he says, "is off!"
"Oh," you say, feeling like a dunderhead,
"never had *that* problem before."

He hangs up

Back down to the cold furnace room
where one spark
could inspire it to make music

You kneel before it
and strike a match
lighting one end of a cardboard taper

This is the altar
this is where the ceremony must begin

You press the red button
Choof!
all twenty-two pipes light up

You feel the surging of water
the transfiguration by flame

You feel the warm booming music begin
an incantation against winter
a hymn to the harnessing of fire

So you thank God and the plumber
and the Peerless Furnace Co.
of Boyertown, Pennsylvania
(less than seventy-five kilometres from Bethlehem)

for these notes of exalted steam
spiralling upward like holy smoke
through tubes that once were cold
as the ice of doomsday

for helping you compose
this psalm of light

for making twenty-two suites
percussive with clangs and whistles

Tenants will stop freezing
plants will stop dying
and you will be able
to return to something
like heavenly sleep

Quietly she strides
to the other end
of the table.
I watch her
peer over the side
to the cold straight drop below.

She's a Royal
typewriter and has threatened
(more than once)
to plunge before my eyes.
She won't accept neglect
even for one day.

Will this be her
next attempt? The floor,
I imagine, is
looking up invitingly
at my errant
and arrogant writing machine.

She demands too much—
my unswerving devotion!
Should I remain a slave

to her pampered keys?
Yet without her
how would I behave?

Helpless,
I reach over

to save
both of us
from destruction.

declines to imbibe your lyrical story.
School switched him off. He won't swallow verses.
Instead, he is a connoisseur of gory
      scenes on his television set, sits immersed
      in images of sweat, men who pummel.
You join him in his spartan territory,
crunch his extra-salty pretzel sticks, guzzle
his beers, spurred by wrestlers spouting feigned glory
      whose rehearsed battles serve him on Sundays.

So you dine with him, and you swim, slowly,
among his bottles, until your eyes glaze
and close during a loud commercial break.

Go on like this: you'll have no more stories
to share...no more poems to make.

POET AS CHRONIC CASE

And some go mystical, and some go mad—A.M. KLEIN

and you become obsessed
with the whole chronicle of obsessions—ANDREW SUKNASKI

CHRONICLING

how chronic is this chronicling obsession
the need to make a poem
out of everyone's living
and everyone's dying
I among them

WEDDING

at my wedding I will dance once
with my smiling bride

then I will crouch
in a corner with my metaphors
tasting words not yet spoken

swirling each simile
like wine on my tongue

testing the unfinished poem
a few crumbs of wedding cake
dark against the roof of my mouth

FUNERAL

I will be the only one
too distracted
to mourn at my funeral
pen in hand I'll remain unobtrusive
scribbling a new image
furtively in the shadows

revising my last lines
among the plot of tombstones
already laid down in my head

SUBVERSIVE ACTIVITIES

There are no activities
more subversive than dreams

1. STOREROOMS

Being excitable
you can be incited to riot
wholly inside your body

nobody will put out
your night fires
or stop you from breaking

into your storerooms
displaying all your past cases
of no goods.

2. STATUES

Within you a city is burning
structures are being turned over
voices screeching in darkness
and vandals pulling down
cold monuments to dead tyrants

these statues within you resemble
fathers as seen by their children
when fathers were bigger
than they actually are

they are threatening still
to destroy from within
with their silent staring eyes
their accusing stances
in stone.

3. PLOTS

No chance

to be rescued from yourself
without taking
yourself down with you

into plots of vegetable calm
into graveyards tended by ghosts

Inside you
where else can you go
for refuge

No place

but somewhere
inside yourself
where you are afraid to go.

THE ANTI-COLA MAN

for laurie block

*a submission for the long-postponed release
of the anti-cola man who had one day refused
to buy into the general madness*

the anti-cola man is enduring the penitentiaries of earth,
is being shuffled from one cellblock to another, is learning
to live with what is minimal: starched garb out of fashion,
pillowless bunks like slabs of ice

sometimes the anti-cola man yearns to die, and is saved only
by remembered simplicities, sunlit images that soak his eyes:
their kitchen table beneath frosted windows where the rays
light up not only the glaze of butter on pancakes but also the
seductive curls of steam from his cracked blue cup of coffee:
now so little to live by but his longings, her scented body
beside him, stroking each other in the dark

the anti-cola man would like to hear again (just once) the
sound of his children laughing, instead of men weeping in
the shadows, but sometimes he is tempted to join the other
damaged goods who curse one another with chapped fists in
each other's faces

what the anti-cola man will take with him if and when he
leaves this latest shivering place: pebbles in his shoes, sweat
under his armpits, bags beneath his eyes (such luggage, after
all, is weightless, but also heavier than a sofa which no man
can carry up a flight of stairs alone)

sometimes the anti-cola man would like to be ushered right
through the gates of heaven, and so he prays: *pity them,*
those stiff-backed men, armed with their corporate directives
of polished glass, yes, pity them, who have exiled themselves
from a deeper knowing

the words of the anti-cola man are thin ribbons passing
through the electrified iron bars at night, streamers
sent out to someone invisible, each sentence a snake
self-released, spiralling toward the stars

THE MYSTERIES OF SEX

Edmonton, 1972

Today, after he reads yesterday's newspaper
in the laundromat around the corner, he trudges home
through the glaring snow, carrying his clean clothes
and the expropriated paper. The stairs creak

to his basement room. On his bed he marks and clips
articles for folders he has labelled ALL ABOUT DREAMS,
THE WORLD & ITS ABSURDITIES, THE MYSTERIES OF SEX,
LEISURE TIME & UNEMPLOYMENT, OLD AGE & DEATH.

When he is through clipping, he deposits the folders
inside his old army surplus steel filing cabinet.
He makes himself supper. Between four slices
of eighty percent whole wheat bread he spreads

some chunky peanut butter and orange marmalade.
Next, one can of Vegetarian Vegetable Soup (condensed)
to which he adds a half can of tap water, heating up
a thick broth. For dessert, a cold Spartan apple.

After this: a hot shower. He stands in the steaming
stall for half an hour, beads of fervent water,
streams of torrid air massaging his back.
The green bar of soap, which smells somewhat

like cinnamon, diminishes to a sliver
before it slips (softly) down the drain.
Then, the highlight of his social season.
He and his latest fling go out to a movie

at a theatre downtown. Afterwards, they ride
the city bus to his favourite pizza parlour.
They share a cheese and anchovies pizza.
Her share: one-eighth. His: seven-eighths.

For conversation they chat ALL ABOUT DREAMS,
LEISURE TIME & UNEMPLOYMENT, THE MYSTERIES OF SEX.
After pizza, he walks with her to the bus stop.
They wait in the falling snow. They stand apart.

He: Maybe we should've had a *plain* pizza.
She: No. I *adore* anchovies.
She steps inside the Number Five bus,
is swallowed by the warm light.

They wave goodbye. Why could he not obtain
even a goodnight kiss? The bus churns from the curb.
Strangers bundle past. He is standing alone
in the falling snow beside a street lamp.

The crystals slanting down resemble commas.
Periods. Semi-colons. Question marks.
But mostly, they resemble asterisks. Those
miniature six-pointed stars that land and dissolve

on his heavy frayed overcoat. Those soft footnotes
plummeting from the sky. He feels like one of them.
Tumbling continually. Never clinging. Melting
into the fine colourless composition of the night.

Although I know God is within me
why am I still
a puffed-up piece of rice?

One day I will throw my cleverness
into the nearest garbage can.
Words brilliantly knotted
cannot tie me to the Word.

I will not be taken in
by scriptural tyrants and slaves
though they pound on the doors of my ears
and break open the sashes of my eyes.
The truth cannot be grasped
simply by turning pages.

The quiet road that carries me
to the capital of heaven
is one never charted
on the changing maps of this world.

"Although the human brain is surrounded by a membrane filled with nerves, the brain itself has no feeling."— Filler in *Regina Leader-Post,* August 24, 1983

Visiting the psychology professor's office, I notice a black and white marble chessboard, the pieces fallen across the squares like toy soldiers. Next to the chessboard, a glass tank lined with darkgreen plastic sheeting, the kind to empty the garbage in. And floating in that clear pool, a brain—a child's brain, its texture yellowish-grey.

"It's pickled," he tells me. "Go ahead. Hold it."

Nervous laughter. I hesitate. "Never touched a brain before!"

"It's not as heavy as it looks," the professor says, grinning.

Now I lift you from the bottom of an alien sea. You are cupped in my palms, dripping formaldehyde. Your rubbery folds, ridges, rivulets once could form a song, or ask your mother, "What's for supper?"—or wake from nightmares screaming.

Who do you belong to now?

I see you will never finger the broken textbook on the professor's shelf, *Studies in Abnormal Psychology,* all that gilded lettering on the binding. I see you will never bathe in the warm water of a family of your own. I see you will never learn how to move the Queen and her forces, threatening the King.

Holding you, I know you will never do anything to save the world from itself.

Disquieted, shivering, I leave the professor's office and step back into the mystery no one can dissect.

My body marches into sunlight, taking a narrow path under arches of yellowing leaves. For the first time I feel every muscle, bone, and organ locked within me. How fiercely now these parts of me embrace each other, beneath my skull's darkened halo.

SOLO

You will have to deal with this one day.
No further postponements:
Wet one finger
and touch it to your chest,
drumming on bone. This is
the final music your body will produce
before someone covers it with a white cloth
to prevent the light from sticking to your skin.

You will escape through the clouds
into the hidden sky.
You must fly
alone, leaving the planet.
At last, you will learn how to sing
without your body's accompaniment.

The Grass Swimmer

The blades look so green and smooth
    I begin to swim across them,
        their coolness rubbing against me.

      As my long shadow strokes through
    the seductive silk meadow,
sunlit reeds smudge and stain
    my arms and legs and belly.

    Quicker than a silver snake
        severing the grasses—
           I ripple past the startled birds,
moving below them like a wave.

I.

I am alone in woods yet not alone,
one visitor among a multitude of hosts.

Trees, birds, small animals, and insects
have made this their green municipality.

2.

On an altar of fallen branches

I rest my body, while you amuse me
with your eight-legged explorations

crawling over the tangled forest of my arm.

3.

Soon I will lift you with a stalk of grass,
return you to your unpeopled world.

But when I leave, I must divide the air,
brush against your webbed universe—

break the strands of light.

A pure spontaneous thread of joy
    passes through me, spinning from my throat
    fearless octaves, quilled articulation.

I serenade best where no bars surround me,
    where earth does not resist my rhapsodies,
    where trees let my tuneful jottings blossom.

I am the plumed stirring of syllables
    blessing light, dust made to be melodic.

What else can I do while I am breathing?
    Wasn't I born to shape the air into notes
    and adorn mute shadows with my exultations?

This peopled planet will remain in need of song
    even when my small winged form no longer finds
    sanctuary in its least tangled thickets.

Ice
clings to branches
where leaves hung in June.

Tonight
not even spiders poke
at shadows on the ground.

A crow
glides down,
folds its wings in snow.

Hurriedly
I walk past

on the path of my own sound

while the clenched hands of cedars
hold back the moon.

they are delicately leaning
on one another: frozen stars of water,
constellations that sparkle at your feet.
you stride through quiet shards as they fall
from the sky's cracked bowl, small ice flowers
shining on the boulevards, petals spread over sidewalks,
one enormous garden covered by a thin white sheet.
you move through tiny miracles of design spun
in a kaleidoscopic tumbler. you walk through grain
from airy fields, each kernel reflecting light
and giving light. you could lose your way
among the many varieties of cosmic wheat.
you step into the bright wardrobes of winter,
microbodies keeping warm inside their chalky coats.
you see how they hug the wind to themselves
and how none can remember what you remember:
the distant hills shimmering green in summer heat.

WALKING THE STREETS OF CALGARY

Summer, 1969

Walking the streets of Calgary
after a summer thunderstorm
you are surprised
by what greets you.

On bridges in the afternoon distance
cars make no sounds at all.
When a door to a car
slams two blocks away
you hear it distinctly.

Even the voices of children
playing on their lawns
sound muted, muffled
by this rolling green,
this skybound place.

Calgary is not a city.
It is a hammock
slung between the hills.

TRANSFORMATIONS OF A HERON

Twilight, English Bay, Vancouver

At first from a distance
he seemed a statue made of steel wire
someone had abandoned on the beach

then a spindly child
who was moving hesitantly
while gazing out to sea

but soon I saw he was a heron
poised at water's edge
his long neck bending over stones

then as I approached
closer still
he turned

and with slow
grace lifted
his awkward wings

throwing his shadow on the air
to become a noiseless arrow
gliding over waves

Stanley Park, Overlooking Burrard Inlet
and North Vancouver, Early Summer, 1969

You sleep, Esse,
on the grass beside me,
your eyelids gypsy moths.

The ships that pass each other
silently churn clouds in water.
I look down at your arms
as they shiver and glow
in the colours of twilight.

You will not let me love you.
Did I ever tell your eyes
how they dream, how they flutter?

Clouds ring the snow-fingered mountains.

Soon I will wake you in the dark grass
and watch as you brush away
a thin veil of dew.

Esse, did I ever tell you
the only light that dims
dims behind my eyes?

the whale is at home
at home in the sea

it is man who stands on shore
staring through haze
aiming his sight
at what he longs to be

the whale is content
but man is not
it is he who slaughters
what he longs to be:

to be a whale
in the green deep water
to be a natural philosopher
in an ocean of philosophers

to be a rolling wet boulder
down the valleys of water
to be one eye open
always toward heaven

this one is made of orange blossoms
an orchard glowing with the sweetest juiciest words

and this one is made of steaming porridge
hot cinnamon oatmeal filling my nostrils
          as I awake in the next room

and this one carries its overwhelming stench
into the back alleys of my brain
a versatile compost pile
of warm earthy scents
that would push away
the most sensitive visitor
to this wild eden /
          perfumed garden /
                    image-strewn backyard

come and sniff these recycled lines
you curious dog,
                    your tail
wagging the aromatic wind

I always see the woman in the moon,
the one who eclipsed the man that others see.
She is a balloon at night among the stars, and drops
out of sight when songbirds wake up to light.

I always see the woman in the moon,
her face chipped away by the growing
shadow of the earth. Still she shines for me:
cool and pristine, a cameo in blue
glowing upon a pebbled field of white.

I always see the woman in the moon.
She circles my bedside with her soothing gaze.
When my body is on fire, when my heart
smoulders, when my soul is steaming, she greets me
at my open window, beckons me to fly
after her, to stroke her alabaster skin.

I always see the woman in the moon
whenever I recline beneath her veil of clouds.
She lingers on my eyelids as she floats by,
her reflection rippling on those thin folds,
her beauty transformed in my brightest dreams
into the eye of a doe, the wing of an owl,
a silent wheel spinning on a bare-branched tree.

We've reached another ledge
of this steep and jagged place.

After years of climbing
and bleeding
                        and groping for roots
we remain
children
            on the edge of space.

            *

Small and thin
these pebbles we have thrown:

to land
                only where we have been

                                to echo
how little we have grown.

            *

The stars bring us comfort
not this stark earthly air

trees being stirred
                        wings
beating without a bird.

*

In full moon light
                    our shadows
resemble giants
hovering near.

Each of us
is a child
                    abandoned here.

*

Sometimes we cloak
                    death in mirth
but with the sun gone
we share the same fear.

We hold each other close
keep the night
                    at a distance.

With the sun gone
only we can warm the earth.

Sometimes The Prairie

Sometimes the prairie hardens lovers
into secret enemies. Sometimes

they declare war on each other's
demanding shadows. Sometimes they
encircle each other with their armies

of ice. Sometimes they make
a truce in darkness, which they sign
with warm forgiving hands.

Sometimes the prairie hardens
lovers. Sometimes lovers bend
like summer grasses toward the land.

Try to imagine mountains
where waves of wheat
resemble oceans
and black soil is richer
than jagged mountain jade.

Try to imagine mountains
with storm clouds
low on the horizon
the sun glowing behind
those dark shapes.

Try to imagine mountains
where every rise of land
is called a hill
and every hill dreams it is a mountain.

Try
to imagine mountains
where there are no mountains
to lean against
for shade.

Paradise distracted me. Its verdant beauty
was only tipped on the edge of things.
I moved in toward the unbounded centre
further from towering mountains,
ever further from the crashing sea.

Slowly I am beginning to wake up,
to find a dreamer's solitude in twilight,
to be continually surprised
by notes of song
performing miracles in my lungs.

I am listening now to a concert of crows.
They no longer bother me
sharing their raucous harmonies with one another.
We are part of the same ecology,
share the same shrine of air.

I walk by scarlet dragonflies
with pollen on their stained glass wings.
They dart into the blue fire of lilac bushes
where they disappear forever.

Twilight lasts longer here
than it does beside the sea.
I never feel as hurried up
as I did when I walked in my sleep

past the glittering boutiques of Paradise
or when I made circles around Lost Lagoon
or strayed among broken seashells
far from the windswept dust of earth.

THE SILENCE OF HORIZONS

*"I liked New York...But then, for me, it grew horizontal—
monotonous."*— JASPER JOHNS, ARTIST, *Newsweek,*
OCT. 24, 1977

Here, on the prairie, day after day, this
horizon becomes the mute accomplice to history.

In one village (population: endangered),
near the only grain elevator, I am shown

a white house abandoned, its front window
crossed by planks. My friend gestures at it,

says the old man who lived there, a widower,
lost his mind, hanged himself inside. A passing

remark. Our soles scuff the gravel road. The green
screen door rattles behind us after we step

inside the general store for some family provisions.
(It is meagrely stocked.) Outside the store, he

shrugs toward the horizon: "Once a man does that
to himself, there is nothing more to say."

I take my time to look. The horizon glows red,
sputters out. The white house slowly darkens.

Nothing grows, not wheat, not hope, out there now.
The wind is collecting you, filling your home
　　With the residue of once-rooted soil.

　　Not even kitchen windows tightly closed
　　Can keep out the endless tides of dust,
Those howling dogs of storm, this barren age.

　　No longer can you separate what you need
From what you don't—spoonfuls of chaff when you must
Breathe air. Your lungs droop inside your bones,
　　Two scarred vacuum bags, dry, draped in a cage.

But in your tumbleweed garden, at least one seed
Is silent somewhere beneath earth's furrowed brow—
　　One seed waiting for your fruitful toil
Seems enough to bank on in your rainsoaked dreams.

This time when he falls
into bed alone
he can smell the Chinese food
clinging to his skin

ginger
fried rice
sweet and sour sauce

He has taken Sing's Café
to bed with him

no drapes of silk and gold
no tasselled lamps
only smiling and frowning faces

Although the glass door
closed on his shadow

he touches the walls again
with the thin film
of his fingers

As he opens his eyes
a scarlet canary
flaps and pecks
outside the steamed window

trying to break in
trying to sing

1. INTENSITY

Finishing my supper. How quiet—
Until the air is—

> Sliced with laughter! Her laughter.

On the phone by the cash register
She gossips in a Chinese dialect.

> Her voice, boisterous. Smoky.

In their corner booth, the owner
Waits for his wife to hang up.

> Fluttering: a deck of cards.

2. INERTIA

I sit alone at the back,
gazing down the aisle of booths.

> Abandoned red flowers.

Beyond the huge front window:
The wind, darkening. Kicking up.

> Gritty spirals and crusty scraps.

I look down at my white plate—
My fork reclined in gravy.

> A swirling cloud.

> The full moon wanes.

in this invasion of grandmothers
how many of you resembled mine

same solemn Slavic features
    (those familiar orthodox Jewish faces)
same strong Ukrainian hands
    (that weathered skin those stout bodies)

and yet I had never seen
a holy army of babas before

you the old women
were wearing your heavy black workshoes
long plain dresses
and babushka scarves
    wrapped like crescent moons
    around your chins and ears

you were pulling together
an old wooden plow
gripped by a man
    over soil and weeds and stones
    digging hard furrows in the field

but especially you
the woman in the lead
straining in your harness
diminutive as an angel
    your delicate bones
    not yet broken

we were told this is how it was
in Old Mother Russia
in the pioneering days
on the Canadian prairies

yes it was only a demonstration
but I witnessed it yesterday
in Yorkton Saskatchewan

and I saw you
the eighty-year-old leader
your white socks falling to your ankles
as you stamped your shoes upon the earth
        the globes of salty sweat
        pouring down your reddened face

and I thought
She's going to have a heart attack
        and I wanted to shout
                        Stop!

but no one would hear me
in the cheering neck-craning awestruck crowd

maybe I was mistaken

maybe this plowing demonstration
is a neglected form of exercise
to be recommended
for all octogenarians
        (of both sexes)

or maybe it's a necessary ritual
of suffering and endurance
preparing us each
for the blessings of heaven

or maybe it's merely
another chunk of evidence
        this crazy world
        is crazy for eternity

O babushkas
O grandmothers
O workhorse angels

O serene old women
serving as substitutes for oxen

tell us the truth

if we never see you again on earth
will this also mark the end
of all babushka plowing demonstrations
in the fields of heaven?

This is the wrong beginning
spring fields
where no blizzards should be

Here the tallest patches of weeds defy
the whitewashed air / here we feel safe
from the fury of flakes
flailing against windows

Plowing past cars bogged down in ditches
we see cattle trying to feed
on a few tufts of grass behind barbed wire

They poke their warm tongues through bright icing
but some give up and move slowly
toward the nearest coulee

Where these cattle huddle
calves may perish
in their new coats of ice
beneath hooves shuddering in storm

The survivors will grow to find
their grassy sunlit world
one day turned upside down
a blow between the eyes

We know an alternative
the only other story possible

the ending / bloodless
some calves found sprawled
and hushed / dreaming in snow

On this icy desert of northern lakes
you step outside into the flawless glare
of an intricate snowed-in afternoon,
the silent scene left over from last night's
long and steady falling full of flakes.

To the horizon from where you stand
it is smooth, except for those places where
the wind scooped out and erased some dark
colours in the earth, making nothing less
than one enormous whitewashed map of land.

In this sculpted air when you hear a dog bark
beneath the high ceiling, the all-blue vastness,
you look straight up, surprised to spot the right
half, the bright half, the ageless white half moon.

I feel like an alien from a desert planet where no one skates, where ice is a mirage, and where the closest thing to pucks are camel droppings. It's my first live hockey game in Canada. Or I should say: my first hockey service.

Here I am sitting on one of the green benches in the bleachers near centre ice under a heater that isn't working, frigid air rising from the cement floor into the soles of my boots. I'm a visitor at the Al Ritchie Memorial Arena in Regina, Saskatchewan. And this is a late night clashing the day after Christmas, 1980.

I huddle among hockey parents, secular worshippers in their community sanctuary. They've come to watch their cherubs in uniform play in the bantam league, the Cougars versus the Lions.

But I'll soon be given reason to believe that it's really the Christians versus the Lions. Because tonight is the night I'll discover: hockey is not exactly in the same league as Sunday School.

On the bench in front of me, a hockey mother makes a verbal appeal for divine intervention: "Knock his *#%+@* block off! Ice th' #*+%$# thing!"

So help me she's got a babe against her breast and—"Where th' hell didja learn ta play this game, ya #*+%$# chrysanthemum!"

This modern madonna, Our Hockey Mother of the Curses, is chewing a wad of gum and holding an unlit cigarette in her free hand. Beautiful.

Another hockey mom is sitting beside me. She hardly says anything, watches silently, one could even say morosely.

Who is enjoying this service anyway?

The young players all look grim and determined, as if they were taking a mathematics exam. Their coaches resemble men who have just lost their jobs and are facing divorce, bankruptcy, and a fatal disease all in one swoop. And the adults in this congregation don't exactly sit there clapping their hands, smiling and laughing, looking serene.

Between the first and second period, nearly everyone leaves the bleachers to get a shot of coffee in a styrofoam cup, or to smoke a cigarette. But this is bantam hockey: no fights, no violence. Not like what I see on television where the heroes of these young guys are all gods who use their sticks and their gloves and their flashing skates to express something other than brotherly love.

To make sure, however, that I don't leave this place with any wrong impressions about hockey's holy appeal and the primary expectations of its devoted worshippers, I watch some older kid not wearing a uniform walk onto the ice immediately after the service is over.

He punches a player in the face.

Hey, it's Boxing Day. Against all ritual the losing team is instructed not to shake the winning team's hands.

Having also achieved the proper spirit of this earthly religion, I frown as I walk out. I feel like I'm leaving a funeral parlour.

I have no illusions. I know this is a sacred sport played and watched in every city and village in Canada. It has winners and losers who all pray fervently for grace and violence and victory.

But now you can see why I'm also assured:

They don't play hockey in heaven.

WHAT IT IS LIKE TO BE THE TELEGRAPHER IN BROOKS

In Memory of Ted Plantos

You are not the telegrapher in Brooks. You are just
a poet and a passenger on the eastbound Canadian as it
chugs through white flakes in the prairie night.

You are the only other customer in the lounge car at this
late hour. You hold a glass of ice-jiggling ginger ale. Seated at
a separate table, he holds a glass of foam-spilling beer served
to him by a compatriot on the line. He begins talking to you
across the aisle about his job as the telegrapher in Brooks.
You listen while this old iron steed puffs its way through the
snowy Alberta countryside three hours late coming into
Brooks.

Chewing on a cheeseburger he informs you why he
doesn't savour Canadian Pacific food: "Doesn't fill the
gaps in my hunger."

The telegrapher serves as the middleman between the
dispatchers in Calgary and the engineers and conductors
aboard the trains travelling in and out of Brooks. Via a
two-way radio and between sips of coffee, he relays to
them the precise location of trains.

The telegrapher in Brooks says he never gets lonely on
the job. He likes the work. He helps prevent accidents along
his section of the line.

Finishing off the last chunk of his Canadian Pacific
cheeseburger he tells you he's engaged to be married to a
social worker in Calgary. And so, three times a week he
commutes between Calgary and Brooks.

Before he gets off the train the telegrapher tells you how he got this job, how it changed his life—"like all things, by accident."

For he was once upon a time a not-too-contented travelling salesman for some firm down east, until a friend of his took the Canadian Pacific Telegraphers Course. And one day his friend told him: "Hey, it's *not* bad work— "

Through the lounge car windows you watch the telegrapher step onto the wooden platform near the black and white sign identifying the town.

Leaving bootprints in the snow he enters the station.

You see a big blue thermos perched on a windowsill. That must be the specially brewed coffee waiting for him in the telegraph room.

You are not the telegrapher. While you gaze at the blue thermos and the old empty baggage cart on the platform, and while the train lets off steam in the middle of the night, and you sit alone in the lounge car with the ice melting at the bottom of your glass of ginger ale, you suddenly wish you were him.

He will be drinking black cups of coffee all through the night talking to his colleagues up and down the CP line and thinking of his fiancée waiting for him in Calgary.

But you are not the telegrapher. You're riding the Canadian and you're pulling out of Brooks. And as the train begins to shake you're stirring a glass of melted ice and thinking about your work.

You are a poet in Canada. Sometimes this means little warmth and no security. You're dedicated to your craft, but you're labouring for no one and doing what no one who's not a poet can comprehend or concede is work.

You are not the telegrapher in Brooks. But you dream that you are. This is your last picture of him:

He is seated at his desk with a cup of coffee warming his hands, probably content not to be struggling over yet another quintessential Canadian poem.

SITTING BEHIND THE WOMAN WHO SMOKES

Summer, 1985

On the bus somewhere between
Fort Qu'Appelle and Yorkton,
I am sitting behind the woman who smokes.

I am trying to understand
why any breathing body
would ever yearn to make
snakes of smoke spout and spin
out of its burning mouth.
What is this mysterious pleasure
some people find in swallowing fire?

I smell the smoke as it twines
around her long red hair.
And I think of *kometa,*
the Greek word for comet:
woman's long-flowing hair.

The comet-haired woman does not know
I am watching her reflection
as it shimmers on the window.

She lifts her eyes from the magazine
spread like a map upon her lap.
Through the white mist of fumes
she gazes out at the passing fields,
the barley and wheat and flax,
the sloughs drying up in the relentless sun.

Now I am beginning to imagine
why the long-haired woman smokes:

– It is her subconscious love of fire.
– Her desire to imitate dragons.
– Her savouring the seductive way
  the smoke spirals out of her mouth
  then curls against the windowpane,
  caressing the glass.

Or perhaps this is why she smokes:

– She is strangely attracted to ashes.
– She is boldly willing to flirt with death.
– She would like to reincarnate
  as a blazing comet.

Spent grey shreds of tobacco float
onto the magazine's glossy pages
and onto her skirted knees.
She stops. Butts out the cigarette
in the silver ashtray beneath the windowsill.

No longer is she the woman who smokes.
No longer does she threaten to burst,
at any second, into flame,
into sparks that would ignite the shadow
gradually growing around her.

It is dusk.
She is just another passenger.
She is now as still as ash.

A few idle unremarkable minutes pass
before she lights another cigarette.

How defiant she is, this woman who smokes!
Taunting the medical odds, shrinking
her lifespan, not caring to claim
a few more years of some hypothetical future—

she's giving her breath to the noxious air
for another moment's glowing pleasure.

By now I suspect at least this much:

– Her nerves are radar.
– She's seeking the taste and heat and smell
   of the stubble fire spreading inside her lungs.
– She's scanning her brain
   for the excitement and drama
   that may quickly release her
   from the utter monotony of solitude.

The uneventfulness of heaven
passes endlessly before her:

   the unassuming farmhouses,
   those sluggish cattle
   huddling in the fields,
   those scrawny horses
   flicking their tails
   as they crop the grasses.

She prefers this ceremony of fire
to doing nothing...feeling nothing.

She is another Joan of Arc.
But one who wants to burn slowly
    while she props herself
    behind a wall of heat.

Now she is nestled in the seat before me,
this exotic bird. I stare at her crown
    of flaming red. I behold
    all of her going up in smoke.

Above the train in Manitoba
the northern lights twist:
two snakes crossing the prairie.

Observation car late at night—
a glow of cigarettes,
red planets in darkness.

In this subdued company
I don't force my lips to speak.
I surrender my eyes to windows.

Moonlit trees, moonlit faces.
I see them talking to each other:
their speech is stillness.

Stillness once was an obscure code.
I would handle words like axes
making kindling for my own warmth.

Now I am among the voiceless.
We speak to each other
with perfect clarity.

Under The White Hood

LOUIS RIEL

Afterwards
his child takes
the hangman's noose

turns it back
into a ball of yarn
and gives away
the threads

These are
the loose ends
of the rainbow
he says

RCMP Barracks, Regina

Pardon me, is it true
Riel was hanged
here on these grounds
ninety years ago today?

He was.
You're not the first to ask.
They come in here and
ask us every day.

And the jail, sir—the gallows?

                    Not a trace.
But for your
information, the exact spot
is sixty feet east of the display.

What's located there now?

An officers' quarters
of grey stone, a backyard,
a few bare trees, a clothesline
and prairie space.

                    No ghost, sir?
No ghost to haunt forever
this bleak unearthly place?

He does not answer
but shuffles through papers
behind the souvenir case.

(An hour later down Dewdney Avenue
riding eastward on the bus,
past Government House and the sign
promoting *The Trial of Louis Riel,*
past the Exhibition Grounds
where annual summer crowds
celebrate Buffalo Days—
I see a tall man in uniform
letting a horse gallop around him
while keeping it in check:

the stallion rears, black
mane flying, circling the man
as the rope tightens
around its neck.)

PILE OF BONES

These wounds want to be healed.
They have always wanted
to be healed.

We walk beside the creek
where the buffalo bones were heaped.
We wear dark glasses to hood our eyes.

Oil streaks the water.
Blood streaks the grass.
We pretend there are no wounds.

THE PLATFORM

The man approaches you in the chill air.
His boots creak on the planks.
Your hands are tied behind your back.

He places a white cotton hood
over your head—after knotting
the noose around your neck.

Now the air you breathe
is warm, your own. Your eyes
vanish behind this mask of snow.

Because your face cannot be seen
nothing is conveyed: your lips,
their silent prayer, the forgiveness

in what they say. But the man's breath
turns hot against your hooded head
before he steps away:

Louis Riel,
do you know me?
You cannot escape from me today.

THE LANDSCAPE

No, you cannot recall that face.
And that voice is faceless now.
His eyes have been blanked out

by the prairie snowscape
he places upon your head
instead of a crown of thorns.

All voices have become whispers
in your final muted storm.
The snow separates their bodies

from your vision. They fear
gazing at eyes that see through darkness.
They are all shadows, nothing more.

And the hangman, how long
has his shadow been waiting
to drape your head in snow?

RED RIVER

Has his ghost returned to haunt you?
The bite of a dog in that voice.
You buggers do not *dare* to shoot me!

Again he cries out from the snow
his disbelief, a white cotton bandage
covering his eyes.

You stand near the blue shadows
of your rifle-holding, buffalo-
coated men, outside the walls

of Fort Garry. The tribunal's
judgement of the night before:
He must die

Thomas Scott must die
for raising his voice and his fist
against your provisional government

for insulting your leadership
for hindering the peace with Canada
for boasting once too often

he would destroy the half-breeds
lead them like buffalo
over the edge of a coulee

see to it the thundering earth
would break
every last one's bones.

You give no last moment reprieve
as you blow your warm breath
into your cupped, shaking hands

and watch his blood spread
a stream over the snow
an image to torture your dreams for years.

THE VOLUNTEER

Fifteen years ago Jack Henderson
spat at your shadow when he says it fell
across the jailhouse door:

Louis Riel, I'll be
the one to put
the hangman's knot under your ear.

He claims you locked him up
in Fort Garry. He swore vengeance
for his compatriot Scott's execution.

True to his word
he has slept with hate his lover
these fifteen years to tell you:

Louis Riel, do you
know me? You cannot escape
from me today.

In how many daydreams has he rehearsed
pulling the lever, releasing
the trap where you, trembling, stand?

For this simple use of his hands
he'll be paid fifty, eighty dollars—
the exact sum is not clear.

He says he doesn't want the money
only the satisfaction
of sending your body straight to hell.

CIVIL SERVICE

That cutting accent may belong
to no man here, the voice
an unseen stranger's

shouting in the Ottawa Valley
echoing across the Laurentian Shield
bridging the Red River near St. Boniface

following the CPR tracks as a whistle
steaming across Manitoba into the Territories
stopping at Regina and becoming a whisper

in your hooded ears. The enemy
is always too busy to meet you.
He will not face you now

only send
his message to you
across the surveyed distances:

Louis Riel,
do you know me? You cannot
escape from me today.

His name does not matter.
It never has. He hounded
you into exile and out of exile

into insanity and out of insanity
into obeying Dumont's call to return
and act upon the grievances of your people

now the people of Batoche, St. Laurent, Prince Albert
now the people of the North-West
Indians, Whites, Metis

into the realization
no grievances would be heard
by indifferent official Ottawa

into exasperation at petitioning the invisible
into desperately leading as David
your people against Goliath

into defiance, into seizure
of stores and rifles
to uphold communal dreams

into civil war with all odds against you
into defeat, into jail
a prisoner before the Queen's tribunal

where as God's servant you implored
for the last time to be heard
the peaceful longings of your people

for a new order on the prairie
beneath the dancing lights of heaven
with the singing spirits of earth

while other God-fearing strangers
disguised by the fashions of the day
tried you at last for the murder of Scott

and called it Treason against Her Majesty
called it Insurrection
and sentenced you

to spend your last moments of dignity
under a white hood on their
dark gallows.

THE BEAST

And this voice may not be human
at all. Haven't you
heard it before, heard it scratching

in the shadows, waiting to stifle you
for serving your vision, heard it
in the wind growing hands like bare branches

promising to smother you
after shrouding your hearing
in one last grotesque whisper:

Louis Riel, don't you know
me? You
cannot escape from me today.

THE LORD'S PRAYER

Remembering your farewell
in Montana one year before
to Father Eberschweiler

and now Father André
weeping nearby, believing you a saint,
while you repeat your true Father's words:

Our Father Who art in Heaven
(Father do You see that tree
on the hill there)

Blessed be Thy name
(Father I see a gallows there)
Thy kingdom come

(and I will hang from it)
Thy will be done
on earth as it is in heaven

(for I have seen
the hour of my own death
and I have seen

a flock
of dark geese hovering
and shadows on the snow).

THE UNDYING

At least half the world
waits for fulfillment
an end to endless dying

while your body plummets
into the valley of shadows
your spirit rises, no part of it broken:

I leave neither silver nor gold
am on the threshold of eternity
I do not want to turn back.

THE HORIZON

What appears to be
a lake sizzling below the sun
will dry up when we reach it.

The fields will crack under our feet.
We say this is an illusion
so we do not have to believe it.

Our science separates us, cuts off
our brain from our knowing heart,
makes us worship at the altar of fact,

finds our children guilty of feeling,
sentences our poets to death
for dreams and visions. By denying our blood

is mixed, too, of pain and rapture,
water and earth,
we see our love also silenced

into fear and hate,
all of us condemned to live
under the white hood, the harsh sky.

This Imagined Garden

for Ernest & Margrith, Catherine & Chad

We lay the rocks on the table
to divide amongst ourselves
like coins after a small robbery.

And, in the candlelight, we calmly examine
some petrified wood, those discarded shards
left among ashes at an ancient campsite.

We pass around one hardened splinter,
hold it before the jittery flame
to see subtle colours translucent as smoky glass.

Imagine ourselves
long-time collectors of earth,
its fragments, its sediment, its plants opalized.

Imagine ourselves becoming stone,
voiceless but shining.

ANNE, DANCING

for Anne Szumigalski, 1922-1999

I want to write something in favour of grace,
the kind that surprises us when we find it.

I am remembering Anne, the poet:
      one orbicular oracle leaping,
an ample ballerina with dainty feet.

I am scribbling a letter to myself
and other poets who are thin and clumsy
to observe and learn from her nimble example:

     What dances
              dances inside of us.
     It's not the flesh we carry
     that frolics with sounds
              but the soul that carries our flesh.

If we step in harmony
to the wordwinds that play within us

     then we may turn as Anne turned
          (alone that night upon the stage)
     into a joyous self-made breeze

     and we may allow
     all in attendance to see
         there are always
         new holes in the air
         for us to leap through
     with the grace of a poet, dancing.

FOR ELI

"the fine surprise that metaphor is" * — ELI MANDEL, 1922-1992

poet, knower, how we devour you
    your omnivorous readers
    how we eat up your words
what your metaphoric body
    desires to swallow and
    be swallowed by
images of earthworms eating
    earthworms children eating their
    fathers eating their children
yes, you love them
    like any earthfather
    sensing something surprising and
off-centre
    gritty and grotesque
    in this compost of love
your earthfather love
    so complicated to express
    even if you are a houdini with words
a sleight-of-mouth artist like me
    burrowing in and out
    of the cold and crushing clay
in the struggle to become
    a master earthworm illusionist
    a gnawer of articulate dirt
a coiled conjurer who composes
    below the alternate rainbow
    in our furrowed soil of verse
        trying to say love
            trying to say
                love

---

* October 12, 1978, in conversation at Regina Public Library, Regina, Saskatchewan

BREATHING IN THE BEES

for Andrew Suknaski

"Listen to us," their wings whisper. "We insist.
We've some sacred images for you."

I'm the poet. They're the uninvited guests,
the spirits of the forgotten and the dead.

They hover above the boxes of books on the floor
and the yellow news clippings cluttering my desk.

They tap on my skull relentlessly, these bees!
They weave through the leaves of my hair.

Soon, some of these intruders sway
on the stalks of my fingers.

What choice do I have?
They won't let me rest.

Once more I permit them to rebuild with words
the honeycombed chambers of my heart.

for Phil Hall and Ann Silversides

1.

You welcome me to your hexagonal garden
as flowers invite bees.

This is not a question
but if it were
the answer would be:

a butterfly
pulsing its wings
slowly, on the warm bricks.

2.

As flowers invite bees
you serve me a glass of iced tea

its amber layers of sugared water
skewered by the sunlight
cool in my hand.

Looking down I point
to the tiniest tendrils of green
rising through cracks in the bricked earth.

3.

As you talk, I lean closer
believing this garden is one place
where metaphors begin

where a poem rises
through cracks in the bricked earth

where the family dog (mane like a lion's)
ambles towards us, each step

hefty with silence.

4.

The only dynasty
is the dynasty of breath.

Within its warm circle
we speak and share our dreams

as the dog with the mane of a lion
settles in one corner's shade

as flowers sway
inviting bees into their sunpierced hearts.

ALL THE YOUNG GREEN PLANTS, ALL THE WILD FLOWERS

for Pat Lowther, 1935-1975

Once one death scars us all deaths scar us.
I do not know why this is.
After that first death...

The newspaper clipping was pinned to my door
the way a grasshopper
had been pinned to the door in my dream.
When I came home and saw the clipping
I felt as if the blow were to my own head
as if someone set out to tear apart
the fibre of the world,
all the young green plants, all the wild flowers.

I could not for those first few minutes
cope with my surroundings or myself.
I stood by the kitchen window looking down
at the alley and the smoothed over lot
where the house next door once stood.
The house had been torn down
just this month, the ground combed over
as if no house had ever stood there.

I felt my eyes lashed with water, seared
with heat like the dying sun: one life I knew,
cared about, shared feelings with, was warmed by—
gone—and other lives preceded, and other lives
would follow. And what did my own life matter
in the accounting, as I spun away from the window
and saw the entire world would one day
be torn down, smoothed
over.

Each time his ear-splintering tirade tolled the hours
the poet, his wife, would secretly take flight.
To evade his body-politicking rage
she would escape where he could not be heard

to the sanctuary of the page
that cool balm of light
where her breath
aspired, blowing smoke rings that broke

against her papered walls, his domestic cage.

Somehow she knew the poetic ticking of each word
would daily mark the postponing of the end.

It was here her heart's blue ink would write—
in this imagined garden, where she would bend
to grow her body's untrodden flowers.

[A Sonnet in Reverse]

In your only letter to me, typed in haste:
"It's life that counts." (Letter and life, both displaced.)

Later why did death hammer a darker light
upon your poems' silken threads, the bright array
your inner life had spun? Why did your being killed
take on more tonnage than your patterns I rejoice?

For poetry, you gave your body, which death erased
with the bluntest instrument. His disgraced
prop. That brute end. But I hear your warm-limbed voice

tiptoe on the earth. You leave my eye transfixed
reading your lines intricate, supple, mixed.
You redesigned the shining air between your life
and death. He thrashed to pull apart your webs. But they
still breathe the brighter ray since you've been stilled.

KNOWING MY POEMS CANNOT SAVE ME

Knowing my poems cannot save me
I drop my heavy suitcase of words

and keep on pacing, looking for wisdom
in the eyes of friends and strangers.

Knowing my poems cannot save me
I awake each day from my travels to heaven,

walk the streets disguised as no one, and find
even the smallest creatures are clothed in light.

from tongue to ear, mouth to mouth
word carries us through
    the bitter tunnels of our throats
        into sudden blinding light,
        the sweet groves of breath—

how word travels
    syllable upon syllable
moving along an endless track,
breaking off into gleaming lines:
    until it's shunted aside
        to catch fire,
        to unshackle water,
    to couple with the wind—

all the passengers of word
gather again at the festive table:
    after so much travelling apart
        we taste this bread, this wine
        passing through our lips—

how word enjoys
its own resuscitation,
    hearing itself resound
in the ever-resurrected air—

Veil

VEIL

[poems of concealment]

"Despite the glories of humanity, it remains a fragile species."
— ELLIOTT LEYTON, *Hunting Humans*

"Sometimes I thought about murdering the whole human race."
— A MULTIPLE MURDERER

HER FACE

in the solemn altar of your house
her face is now the icon lit by candles
smiling from the wall in the living room
framed above the fireplace, across from the sofa
where you and your guests cannot help but see it

and it glows beneath the lamp
on the night table beside your bed

her face small and smudged
in the wallet in your purse
to show in case someone should ask
how're you feeling? are you okay?

and in the glossy magazine
in the supermarkets
her face in the line-up
with those others
tilted for the camera
for the best shot

each one gazing into the future
from the pages of a college yearbook
young and fresh and
taken before

he broke the glass
that protected them
from the grime of the world

yes her face is one of theirs
but you deny it
by refusing to wear
a veil over your own

instead you keep
her face for yourself
for that miraculous night
when she will knock on the back door
and with haunted eyes
collapse in your arms

HER BODY

never found.

something else
no mother could forgive him for.

when you chose to clutch her
in absence, telling your friends
she might still come back tomorrow,
at first they seemed to understand.

when one year, two years, three years crept past
they watched you
keep the curtains closed to all your rooms,
and they stopped asking:
when will you let in starlight
watch the moonrays dance?

now they are stymied like the sun.
none of them can crack
the coat of ice
you have wrapped as a veil
around your body, your house.

HER ROOM

this is how she left it: her dresses hang

in the closet, her shoes are lined up
on the floor. one of her purses lies

open on the dresser, resting beside

her hairbrushes and combs. her perfume bottles
gleam next to her jewellery box
studded with seashells.

you won't
throw anything away. each object is preserved
for her arrival.

              what year is it now?
the calendars have been removed.

everything
is frozen in your house:
her room, your heart, all occasions for joy.

this is how you wait for your daughter's return.

everyone commiserates, everyone tries
to bring you to reality, everyone
tries to reason with you.

they see the invisible veil
over your eyes, the dry film
beyond tears when you look down
at the carpet, closing the door

on each of their faces.
they hear the tremor in your voice
when you suddenly hang
the phone in its cradle

refusing to hear more of their talk
of adjustment, of acceptance,
of learning to give up
her presence, her life with you

to stop believing
her absence is temporary
and at last replace

the hopeless light of your love

with resignation,
the proper balm of defeat

by packing away her clothes,
giving everything that is hers
to charity, closing her closet
and locking up her room

mourning then
this double sacrifice—
hers and yours—

by wearing for them
their undeniable
veil of darkness.

THE RADIO

you can't stop thinking about it
how you were too far away to hear

when he took her from you
her screams muffled
by the radio blasting
inside his car in the woods

while you listened at home
to the radio in the kitchen
and glanced out the window
at the plump robin on the lawn
as it pulled at a worm
to feed its young

whatshisname singing a country song
about jilted love
followed by the latest weather report
(a cooling trend)
then a commercial for diamond rings
on sale at half price

were those the moments he hurt her
when he would not allow her to live?

but you believe she escaped from him

perhaps she was the one he talked about
the one who was too strong for him
although he struck her on the face
the one who struggled with him
and pushed herself out of his car

who is still hiding from him
suffering now from amnesia
wandering, disturbed, in another city
like static far away

THE OFFER

you might have forgotten the incident
until now

she was only four
when you found her

talking to a stranger
in the toy department at sears

he was holding a colouring book offering it to her
when you wrenched her hand away from his. you asked him
what in the world he was doing and he said he thought she
was lost, he was only trying to help. and you said men like
you always say that, i could have you arrested for
kidnapping. and he said there must be some mistake, lady

you pulled her crying and protesting from the toys
and told her not to talk to strange men again

if you had only been there when that other stranger
offered her a lift from campus, you would have warned her.
she would have replied, i'm an adult now mother you don't
have the right to interfere in my life

even if she had yelled it at you
you would have dragged her away

HIS NAME

you say his name does not matter to you
he was always anonymous

even when he enticed each young woman
into his car, even when he

stripped off the veil of civility
and exposed the blank sheet of his face

this erudite and articulate man
who crumpled each innocent coed

one at a time, in city after city, year after year,
and threw them away like crushed beer cans

this man who remained anonymous
until someone

identified him and arrested him
and judged him and sentenced him and

erased him,
like a spelling error.

HIS PLEASURE

at first they whispered
the worst thing he did to you
was take away your only child
take her away from you forever

now they whisper
the worst thing
he did to you
was murder you

like this, every day

you,
one he never touched
never met, never considered
for a moment, even while

he took her body and covered it
with dirt and leaves
to hide his pleasure
bury his fear

he believed
he was the only one
who really mattered

you have learned
any man who slays
a single soul
murders a multitude

so
that he
cannot slay you

you must
keep her
alive

THE CELL

you will not tell them
your nightmares
your forbidden dreams
like the one where you spend
some time with him
in his narrow cell
his hands tied
with a yellow clothesline
behind his back
while you clutch a knife
you took from the kitchen drawer
in your cell next to his
but the guard
grabbing your arm
just before you lunge
has pudgy dirty fingers
and it is he
who chokes your curse

THE POOL

and there are other nightmares

you and your daughter
swimming at the local YWCA

you smile at her
as you dogpaddle
in the shallow end

suddenly an iceberg
(where did it come from?)
juts up in the deep end

it separates
you from her
dragging her beneath
the blue shimmering water

you struggle to reach her

when you wake up
you're calling out her name
screaming, trying to save

the two of you
from drowning

THE SCREEN

she's the only one you really want to talk to

but she is somewhere
behind the screen

you sit in front of it every night
watching the news

although every door is double-locked
every curtain closed
the screen is continually bringing
another murder into your house

you see one more corpse
covered with a sheet

in the living room darkness
someone is always
stabbing you in the heart

the bloodletting never stops
the ambulance
arrives too late

while they're trying to revive you
the revolving red light
flashes in your face

you can't tell anymore
if you're dead or alive

her silence
has become

your shroud

YOUR BREATH

now your friends
may begin to understand
to be tortured once like this
is to be tortured forever

now they may grasp the truth
you are not a survivor
but one more victim
leaving no traces of blood

now at last they may see
through the veil covering their eyes
how her absence
has stopped your life

now they may acknowledge
what happens at night
when at last you fall
bruised into bed

how you imagine *him*
throwing himself
upon your body in the dark
the stench of corpses on his breath

it is your breath
he wants to take away

YOUR LIFE

kick him out, they plead, kick him out
of your house, your head, your life.

they have cried for you and you
have cried enough, you have suffered

enough. unfold
a map and go

where your finger lands.
yes. pack up a simple flight bag. yes

and someone will go with you
someone will be there with you

to help you break through
the veil of clouds

to help you
leave death behind.

Luminous Plumes

WITH OUR ATOMIC FATHERS
IN THE ALAMOGORDO DESERT
A FEW HOURS FROM LOS ALAMOS
AND THE SANGRE DE CRISTO MOUNTAINS
WITNESSING TRINITY, JULY 16, 1945, NEAR DAWN

At last we stand silent at the birth
of our first conception,
before the light of our inspiration:
to see our own first son rise
brighter than the sun itself.

We see the tower, that imposing
steel hulk, as it cradles our offspring
who curls into vapour and cries
to embrace the arms of zero.

We see the shocked veins
in our fertile hands
shiver and glow.
Right through ourselves we see
the fragile bones of earth.

White-haired, sandalled, in his blue
and grey robe salted with symbols
of infinity, he stands
on the desert alone, the distant
hills eroding rapidly

A single bead of sweat
drips down his brow:
a moment or a millennium?

He takes the bead, cups it
in his palm, there the water
sparkles, in its convex
reflection he sees the hills
eroding, the sun accelerating
its own dissolution

In the single bead he can see
all this and his own brow melting,

while the wings of a firebird
burn the hinges behind
his once cloudless vision

A dryness forms on his lips,
a bitterness is bestowed on his tongue,
as the bead that fell
into his palm
dissolves

He closes his eyes, drops
to the hot sand, and coils
into a spiral

On the desert all that remains,
all that ever was

a pyramid of smoke

an eye
glowing without a body

flaming feathers
falling from the sky.

CARNIVOROUS HORSE: 1967

I.

Yesterday the cow jumped over the moon
and today we will rocket that cow
not only over the moon
but past the sun.

And when it returns from this historic trip
we predict it will be
the first bovine on earth
to give birth to a litter of giraffes.

And tomorrow we plan
to melt mammoths from the ice age
to determine how well they can survive
while facing the traffic on our paved highways.

And tomorrow we will spawn a horse
able to digest the flesh of other horses.

2.

Tomorrow further experimentation calls
for the accurate positioning
of a series of intricate mirrors
halfway between the earth and sun.

We will angle these polished surfaces
from our control centre
in the upper stratosphere.

Then we will shield our eyes
and eagerly stand back
as a bevy of burdensome cities burns.

    Desert scene: polar bears
       sneaking past a cactus.

     In the distance,
  a hummingbird roars.

[main feature]

Hitler's favourite movie was *King Kong*. Likely he sympathized with the gorilla. I can picture him crying at the end, like a ten-year-old candy bar chewer, when King Kong stood atop the Empire State Building swatting at the pesky pilot flies buzzing at his brain (trying to do him in, aiming to bring him down).

I see Eva Braun passing him her hanky, saying, "Adolf! *Meshuggener!* Blow your stinking nose!" and Adolf accepting her hanky with a muffled *danke schön,* then dabbing at his moustache, soaked in genuine tears.

Except I couldn't forget the nature of his sympathy, beyond a ten-year-old believer in the underdog, beyond forgiving the gorilla his destruction because he was snatched from his enchanted isle and forced to exist in an alien world.

No, Adolf must have seen in the movie something more, and he probably saw the movie at least a dozen times sitting there in the dark in his underground theatre wishing in his pure Aryan mind that in the showing this time the gorilla would get his chance to destroy more than half the city (men, women, streetcars) before the rolling of the last tragic reel.

I imagine Adolf deeply moved by the film's injustice (while all of Berlin was being bombed): King Kong never allowed to complete his avenging deeds.

[trailer]

Hitler's favourite movie was *King Kong.*
Laurel and Hardy left Stalin in stitches.
And Mussolini must've got a kick
out of Buster Keaton.

Now here's enough material
to make a movie out of a book:
the simple fact murderous men
are only human

as long as they remain
in their seats
munching buttered popcorn,
drinking Coca-Cola,

laughing, cringing,
wiping tears from their eyes,
and leaving all the Lights,
Camera, Action to the likes

of *Dr. Caligari*
and *The Phantom of the Opera,*
to sweet little Mary Pickford
—and the Keystone Kops.

could raise
vodka glasses
to the ceiling

could move
       bishops
           and pawns
across squares

could crush
       skulls

and then

       caress
a daughter's curls

[Revisions of a Dictator]

"To choose one's victim, to prepare one's plans minutely, to slake an implacable vengeance and then to go to bed...there is nothing sweeter in the world."— Zozo

ZOZO

Their three other children had all died in infancy.
He was the one who survived.

His father was a failed cobbler.
The man drank heavily
and enjoyed the thrashings
he gave his only surviving son
in their two-room shack in Gori.

The boy was small, bright-eyed, clever.
He was eleven years old when his father died.

His mother, a washerwoman, was very pious
and completely dedicated to her precious son.
She worked overtime to help support him.
And she gave her boy a sweet name.
Called him Zozo.

The child's real name was Joseph.
Joseph Vissarionovich Djugashvili.

Eventually he would give Mother Russia a thrashing
as he controlled her 800 million unruly people
for nearly a third of a century.
Among her citizens, he would, sooner or later,
eradicate one of every forty.

But only the disobedient ones.
The treacherous ones.

Sweet little Zozo.

EDIT

Take this as many ways as you want.

As the first editor of *Pravda,* Zozo learned how to edit *the truth.*

He taught himself how to revise history: his own story, the story of others: how he came to power.

To invent fictions about himself he merely needed to call them facts. He would even reward himself with roles he had never filled. (Did you know he was Lenin's chief assistant during the October Revolution? You didn't? Ah, Lenin also didn't know.)

To correct words on sheets of paper proved to be the training ground for Zozo's later editing of lives.

To turn the pages of his chronicles, to alter the face of dialectical materialism, he applied his own Proofreaders' Marx:

Elevate a letter or word.
Sink or depress a letter or word.
Straighten ends of lines.

Carry farther to the left.
Carry farther to the right.
Close up entirely.

All those bloodless gestures.
Performed in ink.
Modifying mistakes.

Starving the peasants of Ukraine
when they wouldn't bow to collectivized farming.
Millions of lives. Corrections on paper.

Delete.
Take out.
Remove. Expunge.

Signing a peace pact with his enemy Hitler,
then rebounding after invasion, to save Russia.
More corrections. A greater toll in lives.

Wiping away errors.
Erasing flaws.
Eliminate. Liquidate. Purge.

Even Nadya, his second wife, finally
could not bear all his revisions
of innocent peasants and loyal comrades.

One night, in her bedroom, she
deleted herself
with a bullet to the head.

More than ink is wiped off
the wet sheets
of corrected history.

OSIP

Zozo feared nothing so much as metaphor.
The unnerving poetry of dissent.

Portrayed in one poem: *His fingers fat as worms.*
I'm another poet who remembers those hands

raising a rusted scythe
to cut Osip, the poet, down.

Now that brazen poet sleeps
under a frozen field of words.

The iron train shakes in passing—
and his bones resound.

*[Verses Based on Texts, Subtexts & Imaginings of the Recorded
Life & the Unrecorded Death of Osip Mandelstam, 1891-1938?]*

NOTES ON MANDELSTAM

1.

Anything can be poured into a poem
      as long as it smells of life
      or reeks of death or stares down
like the cold half moon

2.

Pack all you know into the fewest lines
        the only baggage you're allowed
     to take with you
into exile, into darkness

3.

truth
is dangerous
     poems
     are dangerous
         you can
         die for poetry

THE POET, ARRESTED

"All night the police searched the apartment.
They were looking for poems."
— ANNA AKHMATOVA

Nadezhda Mandelstam, author
and wife of Osip, the poet:

Long after the poetry police rang the doorbell,
long after they first arrested him, we swallowed
what we could of his most memorable lines.
But that night, sitting among our apartment's
vandalized shadows, we had not yet learned
how to keep in the secret corners of our flesh
Osip's unflinching words about this wolf-fanged century.

Showing their unspeakable fear of literature's power,
the poetry police waited for the first glittering
shards of daylight before they escorted him away.
Hope and devotion: these I counted among
the undeclared articles we could take with us
into our exile...into his death.

Somewhere in Siberia the poet's body was dumped
into the earth. Anonymous. Irretrievable.
And everywhere in transit I saved
the forbidden bundle I had rolled up for years—
Osip's unpublished poems, tucked cold
in the handle of an iron saucepan,
never far from my fortress heart.

OSIP'S LAST POETRY READING

1.

inside our transit camp in the Siberian far east,
in the otherwise dismal loft of one of our barracks,
up there as far away from the icy ground
as prisoners could climb to breathe and sleep,
none of them yet quarantined with typhus—

in that privileged loft the only heat
and light that Arkhangelski
and his fellow thieves could muster
was provided by a single candle on a barrel—

and by the warm bodies of his four cronies
and by the rude figure of the head thief himself
(whom even the camp commandant
in order to keep the peace
would have some occasional dealings with
and listen to with due respect)—

together, these cramped and coughing silhouettes,
this reek of bones and ragged flesh—
just like the rest of us,
not so easily recognizable now as men—

summoned me, Mandelstam, the dying poet, to recite
some of my verses, rumoured to be as bright as flames—

this entertainment in exchange
for a portion of scarce white bread
to be dipped into an open tin
which contained some kind of meat—

probably dog food for the pets of commissars—
but no matter, it was for now
the camp's gourmet snack—

and so my last audience on earth
consisted of Arkhangelski and his fellow thieves
common criminals, the true appreciators
of my outlawed lines—

my shadowy brothers whose hunched bodies,
while I spoke, swayed feverishly
on the frosted walls—

2.

now contrast this and that:
my last illegal and paperless reading
in a prison camp thousands of miles from the Kremlin—

and our subdued apartment five years earlier
that spring evening of my first arrest
in circumspect and civil Moscow—

when the poetry police displayed
such trained thoroughness and authorized delicacy
in the way they gathered, piece by piece,
my various papers that had been scattered
throughout our apartment by Nadia and me
on shelves, in books, in drawers, in boxes—

in the way they dropped each of my writings
in the middle of the floor, then, seemingly oblivious,
walked over my life's work, back and forth,
all through the night and into the morning,
while adding more and more papers to the pile—

I still recall that fratricidal site:
my boot-marked poems on the floor,
those rubber-stamped signatures
of Stalin's cool collaborators—

so unlike the merging
luminous plumes of breath
exhaled by my last authentic listeners—

the souls who huddled for warmth in a barracks loft
one winter night in Vtoraya Rechka,
outside Vladivostok, not far
from the grey and grinding sea—

OSIP'S FINAL STANZAS

"The data on his death has not been established. And it is beyond my power to do anything more to establish it."—
NADEZHDA MANDELSTAM, LAST WORDS IN *Hope Against Hope*

Companions

A contagion of spotted typhus—
No, a contingent—
Recently visited our camp—and needed
Warm companionship as much as I did.

So I obliged. The contingent obliged.
We sleep together, uneasily now—

Feverish companions, sharing our dreams,
Our mutual unrestrained hallucinations.

Fever

A damp fervent chill embraces me.
In the dark I whisper to it:

In what dreamlike way
Will this love end?

Chronicle

I catch my breath, I suck in air, I know
Nothing at all about the private history
Of this camp infirmary's public bed,
The steel cot into which I, fevered, fell.

Who died in it first? I want to know!
Who will be the one to breathe in it last?
I would like to chronicle the final days
Of the many frail ghosts preceding me

Stamped out by time on this ill bed. But time
Slowly drains out of me, in watery stools,
In bloody rivulets. Time cannot wait for what
I will soon run out of—ink, wit, food, air.

Bread

Our daily bread is rationed here—
Along with the paper bones of the dead
Allotted to the dogs on the edge of camp.
Our scraps of flesh, our unpenned lines.

The partitioning of bread, of words and lives—
I've become a rational expert in such rationing:
I observe the small portions of each commodity
As they gradually dwindle into crumbs of nothing.

But such precious crumbs, crisp crumbs, crumbs
To haggle over—all disputed crumbs, worth dying for!

Production

When and how do I expect to die? Perhaps,
Since they euphemize death in our detached
But ideal people's state, I shall merely "expire"
In my own bunk, quietly in our quarantined hut.

Or I shall be forgotten, one day left outside
To bask in the arctic air, to bathe and steam skyward.

I admit it, I have become too attached
To my ice-cold barracks. I and the other
Guests of the state appear as shoddy characters
Who drift in and out from the darkened wings
In our Benevolent Leader's endless play.

What more can be revealed about this pantomime,
Our unappreciated production in this obscure
Corner of Siberia? No one familiar to us
Sits in the audience to view our performance.
Non-existent, never promoted, our grim drama
Won't be reviewed by any Moscow critic far away.
And my role in it is kept small and silent.

Let me approach the truth of this glacial scene:
What can the world say to a poet when his words
Are authorized not to be read, not to be heard?

In Transit

This transit camp? Haven't our lives always been
Spent in transit? And, Nadia, haven't I paced
The smallest apartments, rooms, and cells
As if I were striding across the tundra?
Only to come up against these natural barriers—
Frozen lakes, ice—blocked foreboding rivers—
Obstacles no poet is allowed to leap across
Unless he wishes, finally, to drown himself.

Broken Rocks

Until I became too obviously sick
After arrival, I was forced for a time
To do menial tasks like everyone else.
Although I could not help construct
A new barracks for our ever-increasing
Camp population, one night I cleaned,
On numb and bony knees, our latrine.
And I cleared snow—just once—then collapsed.

But the heaviest work I ever did,
Perhaps only in a fevered dream,
Was to lift a pile of broken rocks
And cart them away in a barrow.
Every time I stooped to toss
Each jagged rock, I recognized
Our Kremlin wild man's face—
Crumbling, it made my task less onerous.

What do the authorities do with these
Prolific rocks broken by discarded men?
One pile is transferred to make another—
And the next day transferred back again!
This Promethean task corresponds
To burying bodies, then digging them up
For continual reburial somewhere else.
Men and corpses, who jots the difference?

But the cold earth is cracked open
Again and again, violated so often
I swear I sometimes hear it groaning.

It groans in the dark while I try to sleep—
While I yearn for dreams of abundant seeds
In grey landscapes sprouting glorious green.

In Exchange

I am the poet in the ragged yellow coat—
How my fellow prisoners recognize me.
Some of them worry about me, draw me aside.
They scowl: "Osip, you are skin and bones!
You look terrible! You should be eating more!"
But the soups are thin, the meat meagre

And the leeks and potatoes are too salty, and I
Suspect the guards are trying to poison me.
They do not like poets. They only respect
Murderers and thieves. I count some thieves
Among my friends. They steal bread for me.
I recite my poems for them. I barter to survive.

I barter words, lines, stanzas, in exchange
For metaphors composed from grain, tasty
Symbols of substance. And so I contribute
In a sonorous way to prisoner morale—
I thrive for awhile on such fevered bargaining.

Someone, I am now certain, will see to it
My yellow coat will not be buried with me.
I will wear out long before it does. (Yes,
Let us make use of things. Let us be practical!)

As for my unfinished poems, the ones
I still hoard in the shadows of my skull,
I fear they will all be ditched with me
In exchange for silence by this frosty regime.

What animal are you? You pursue me
in my dreams, waiting to devour. You
track my skin with your fevered air. You
distress my sleep as your night frost seeps through.

I'm stranded somewhere wearing this cloak of clouds,
in some secret land where my bones will be strewn.
My lungs are billowy, bellowing for breath, so I
might wake to pant through this icicled dew.

Within me the superior sun and the wave-tossed sea—
both bless miracles no less momentous than breath.
But winter is imminent and shaped like a wreath:

My seamstress sews the stars onto shrouds,
her laced fingers singing, sparring with the moon,
needles of light stitching the holes in the sky.

One: breathing

I was not a poet when I moved to Vancouver, Canada, at age 25 in November, 1965. I was an American draft dodger, one of the initial protesters against the Vietnam War. But a few months after landing here, I wrote my breakthrough poem and my first published in Canada, in *Talon* magazine, September, 1966. I was an unknown poet accepted by the editor, Jim Brown. In that issue, which cost only 40 cents, I found myself among other beginners, including Patrick Lane, Seymour Mayne, Barry McKinnon, Helene Rosenthal, David Phillips, Raymond Fraser, Tom Marshall, and bp Nichol.

By then I had learned how much I liked to be surprised by words: the way they nestle against each other to sing among themselves; the way they glitter when they combine, producing sparks of radiance; the way they build images of a deeper reality than I encounter every day; the way they engage my soul with their notes of felicity, their spells of ferocity.

Poetry is the breathing gift of light and sound that I pluck sometimes from the silent net of surrounding darkness. Poetry is not poetics. Poetics is a formal reflecting on the idealized event of the poem. Poetics is the discourse about the meal after the meal is over. It's not the food itself. Poetics tells us nothing about how to prepare the next meal, how to make the next poem. It is secondary to the poem and never paramount. For the poet, imagination has no built-in limitations, whereas poetics is self-limiting: it cannot create any of the poems it admires. It may sanction the producing of its theories, but its theories cannot reproduce the passion and sweat of making poems. I've yet to find the poetics that can explain exactly how I've written any of my poems.

Two: expression

To write the raw draft, the first version, of a poem is, for me, not a cold deliberate act—it feels more like a fevered spontaneous expression.

This is the exact opposite of what Wordsworth described as "emotion recollected in tranquility." I never feel tranquil when I begin writing a poem, nor am I serene at any stage when rewriting it. If anything, "composing" a poem cannot be done when one is feeling "composed." Putting a poem together has less to do with relaxation than it does with coming into an eloquent engagement with otherwise inarticulate matter and with the complex causes of tension in the mind, body, and spirit of the poet. Some poems may enhance a state of serenity in the reader, but this is precipitated by the poet's struggle.

What Wordsworth—as poetician, not as poet—was talking about was his peaceful pastoral ideal, his personal poetics. Fine. But his statement that poetry is "emotion recollected in tranquility" grew into an academic truism, joining other paperweight terms, like Keats' "Negative Capability" and Eliot's "objective correlative"—each one adopted as a cover for, or an evasion of, the origins of poetic creation, which remain mysterious and holy and elusive as ever.

In retrospect, maybe it's fortunate that when I was a student of literature at university, in Indiana and California, I was supposed to read and analyze poems, not write them. I became a poet *after* I moved to Canada—ironically, once I freed myself from the "land of freedom," the sovereignty of the Selective Service and the friendly grasp of my local draft board.

Three: re-visioning

It's difficult to sustain that initial excited state beyond the first draft.

But while re-visioning is not often spontaneous, it's not systematic either. The follow-through, the work that I feel must be done on a poem—that's the toughest part of my job as poet. First the draft, then the craft.

My poetic craft is always being tested and challenged anew by multiple problems (here I get technical): problems of structure and contextual details, of phrasing and cadence, of imagery and figurative language that I must resolve and harmonize in each particular instance and in some unprescribed, unprecedented manner if a poem is to merit being called an original work of art.

Until I achieve some satisfactory resolution, I do not believe a poem is ready for the world. And at least half of the previously published poems in this collection have been re-visioned, because I was not totally satisfied with their initial appearance.

My poetry is still developing and expanding within the liberation zone of the re-visioning process. My personal poetics is practical and consists of elements and techniques that are fluid and malleable. It would be wrong for anyone to presume that I operate under some deliberate system, following a rigid doctrine of principles, applying a pre-programmed set of technical resources, while governed through it all by cold reason and brute force.

I'm not a computer. I'm an unfinished human being with an imagination and a conscience. Yes, I am conscious of what I'm doing and what I'm using, but I am not too conscious.

I feel much closer to the unmapped universe of dreams, to the uncodified creative experiences of many of my peers, those poets who are still living and those who preceded me, than I do to the methodical theories of doctrinaire poeticians.

I live and work and play in the final wilderness. I enter it every day. I take it with me wherever I go. It does not belong to me alone, this inner world. I believe within each of us resides the divine—human, animal, natural, supernatural—and it awaits our attention and interpretation and awe, as it transmits through us old messages, new dreams.

Yorkton, Saskatchewan, 2001

THE BOOKS

– from *Moving In From Paradise* (1976)
All the Young Green Plants, All the Wild Flowers
Journey Into Silence
Louis Riel
The Mountains of Saskatchewan
Moving In From Paradise
Sixty Feet East of the Display
Subversive Activities
Under the White Hood

– from *Children on the Edge of Space* (1977)
The Alien
Children on the Edge of Space
Einstein's Brow
I Am Looking North
My Typewriter Contemplates Suicide: 1967
Northern Woods
Transformations of a Heron

– from *The Blue Pools of Paradise* (1983)
Capturing Fireflies
A Document of Secrets:
   I. Of Names and Numbers
   II. Of the Unknown and Unseen
Early Development
The Fabled Blue Pools of Paradise
In My Room: Vancouver
My Great Aunt Sarah's Treasure
The Names Leave the Stones
Poem Beginning with a Phrase by Kandinsky
Seedlings

– from *Listening to the Crows* (1983)
In Woods*
Sometimes the Prairie

– from *From My Box of Dreams* (1986)
Knowing My Poems Cannot Save Me

– from *Lit Like Gold* (1988)
With Our Atomic Fathers...*
You Walk Through Galaxies

– from *Sleeping Among the Pumpkins* (1990)
Heart
Her Rocking Chair*
Nursing Home
Shelf Life
Sing's Café, Yorkton
Stalin's Hands
Variation on a Poem by Kabir

– from *Junkyard of Dreams*(1992)
For Eli*
Solo*

– from *Breathing in the Bees* (1994)
Breathing In the Bees

– from *The Silence of Horizons* (1996)
Notes on Mandelstam
The Poet, Arrested
The Silence of Horizons
With a Few Sips of Green Tea

– from *Rainbows in the Dark* (1998)
Strokes*

OTHER NEW POEMS

---

* *These chapbook poems are published in book form for the first time*

ACKNOWLEDGEMENTS & PUBLICATION HISTORY

The poet takes this opportunity to extend deepest thanks to the publishers and editors of my six poetry books: publishers Bob Currie, Gary Hyland, Barbara Sapergia, and publisher and editor Geoffrey Ursell; publisher and editor Jim Brown; editor (the late) Brenda Macdonald Riches; publisher Gordon Shillingford; and editor Catherine Hunter. Catherine's task for this particular collection was especially demanding—hundreds of my poems to read through! Her fortitude and discernment helped fit many of the best of these together thematically to our reciprocal satisfaction.

Many of the poems selected for this book have been previously published, some in a different form, some under alternate titles. The remaining poems are published here for the first time.

The majority of poems first appeared in the following books, chapbooks, anthologies, and periodicals, or were initially broadcast.

BOOKS: *Moving In From Paradise,* Coteau Books, 1976; *Children on the Edge of Space,* Blue Mountain Books, 1977; *The Blue Pools of Paradise,* Coteau Books, 1983; *Dark Halo,* Coteau Books, 1993; *Variations on the Birth of Jacob,* The Muses' Company/J. Gordon Shillingford Publishing, 1997.

CHAPBOOKS (all published by Waking Image Press): *In the Dark the Journeyman Landed,* 1971; *Adventures of the Midnight Janitor,* 1972; *Children on the Edge of Space,* 1973; *Game Farm,* 1975; *Walls,* 1977; *Aurora,* 1980; *Listening to the Crows,* 1983; *From My Box of Dreams,* 1986; *Lit Like Gold,* 1988; *Sleeping Among the Pumpkins,* 1990; *Junkyard of Dreams,* 1992; *Breathing In the Bees,* 1994; *The Silence of Horizons,* 1996; *Rainbows in the Dark,* 1998; *How Word Travels,* 1999; *The Anti-Cola Man,* 2000.

ANTHOLOGIES AND TEXTBOOKS: *Draft,* Turnstone/ECW, 1981; *The Dry Wells of India,* Harbour, 1989; *Following the Plough,* Black Moss, 2000; *I Want To Be the Poet of Your Kneecaps,* Black Moss, 1999; *Jumbo Gumbo,* Coteau, 1989; *Lines,* Ekstasis, 2001; *No Feather, No Ink,* Thistledown, 1985; *Number One Northern,* Coteau, 1977; *Open Windows,* Quarry, 1988; *Our Fathers,* Rowan, 1995; *Out of Place,* Coteau, 1991; *Ride Off Any Horizon,* NeWest, 1983; *Sky Striders,* Nelson, 1985; *Smoke Signals #2,* Saskatchewan Writers Guild, 1977; *A Sudden Radiance,* Coteau, 1987; *Sundog Highway,* Coteau, 2000; *That Sign of Perfection,* Black Moss, 1995; *Thirty Nine Below,* Tree Frog, 1973; *Three Kernels of Popcorn,* Scholastic, 1999; *Waking Image Bedside Companion,* Waking Image, 1982; *Whale Sound,* J.J. Douglas, 1977; *Where the Voice Is Coming From!,* Vol. III, Saskatchewan Writers Guild, 1994.

PERIODICALS: *Black Apple,* 1991; *blewointmentpress poverty isshew,* 1972; *Briarpatch,* 1976, 1988; *The Canadian Forum,* 1968, 1970; *Canadian Literature,* 1983, 1989; *The Carillon,* 1975; *Chautauqua Review,* 1984; *CV2 (CVII),* 1976, 2001; *FreeLance,* 2001; *Grain,* 1992, 1995; *Intrepid,* 1969; *The New Orphic Review,* 1998; *112th. Street Poetry-People Rag,* 1971; *People's Poetry Letter,* 1995; *Prairie Fire,* 1997; *Prairie Journal of Canadian Literature,* 1987; *Prairie Messenger,* 1988; *Sundog,* 1975; *Talon,* 1967; *Three Legged Coyote,* 1982; *Transition,* 1990, 2000; *Warm Poets for Cold Nights Poetry Sheet #2,* 1975; *Wascana Review,* 1983; *Weekend Magazine,* 1977; *Western Producer Magazine,* 1976.

BROADCASTS: From 1969 through 1973, CKUA AM-FM, Edmonton, aired many of the author's earlier poems included in this book, on the programs: *Is the World Ready?, A Soft Bomb Behind the Eyes, Stand Tall on the Rubble Pile, Poetry and Prose,* and *Night Bombardment.* From 1977 through 2001, some of these poems also aired on CBC Radio's national network programs *Anthology, Ideas,* and *Definitely Not the Opera.* CBC TV featured "To Be a Whale" on David Suzuki's *Science Magazine* in 1978. From 1983 through 2001, many of the poems in this collection were broadcast on CBC Radio Saskatchewan's radio arts programs: *Ambience, The Arts Wrap,* and *Gallery,* as well as on *The Morning Edition* and *Saskatchewan Weekend.* In 1999, three of these selected poems were read by the poet for Saskatchewan Communications Network's *A Literary Moment.*

AUDIO TAPE: In 1998, *East Meets West* was released by Three Morphs Productions in Toronto, featuring the voices of the late Ted Plantos and Mick Burrs (Berzensky), each reading from his own work. Of the 19 "West Side" selections, 13 are included in *The Names Leave the Stones.*

NOTE: "Poet's Afterword: The Final Wilderness" is a reworking of an essay on his own poetry and poetics first published by the author in *The New Orphic Review,* Volume 1, Number 2, Fall 1998.

ABOUT THE AUTHOR

Steven Michael Berzensky has published five books of poetry, and no less than 24 chapbooks of his work, in the last three decades. His most recent publication, *Variations on the Birth of Jacob,* received the 1998 Saskatchewan Poetry Award, while his 1983 poetry collection *The Blue Pools of Paradise* won the Saskatchewan Writers Guild manuscript award. As well, his poems have appeared in nearly 40 anthologies and numerous literary periodicals. A former editor of *Grain* magazine, he also has a half-dozen book editing credits to his name, and has even done cover art for several publications.

Born and raised in California, Mick Burrs, as he is also known, moved to Canada in 1965 and to Regina in 1973. In 1985, he took up a position as the first writer in residence in Yorkton, Saskatchewan, and has lived there ever since.